Making Information Systems Work

Critical Skills for Managing Technology in Organizations

Dr. Macedonio Alanis

Tecnológico de Monterrey

Imprint

Any Brand names and product names mentioned in this book are subject to trademark, Brand or patent protection and are trademarks or registered trademarks of their respective holders. The use of brand names, product names, common names, trade names, product descriptions, etc. even without a particular marking in this work is in no way to be construed to mean that such names may be regarded as unrestricted in respect of trademark and brand protection legislation and could thus be used by anyone.

Cover image photo by Marvin Meyer on Unsplash.

ISBN-13: 9798373086448

ASIN printed version: B0BRLZ3Z57

ASIN e-book: B0BRXXZYK3

https://www.amazon.com/-/e/B08529L1PZ

alanis@tec.mx   maalanis@hotmail.com

Dedication

This book is dedicated to my parents, family, and teachers. I can't ever repay you for what you have done for me. I can only pay it forward.

Acknowledgements

For years, I have been fortunate to interact with professionals who seek to improve the world by taking advantage of information technologies. Many have shared their experiences and guided me in projects in public and private organizations. To all of them, my thanks, respect, and admiration.

I would particularly like to thank my colleagues and my students at Tecnológico de Monterrey, but also at Universidad Ana G. Méndez in Puerto Rico, Universidad del Externado de Colombia in Bogotá, Universidad Autónoma de Tamaulipas in Nuevo Laredo, Carnegie Mellon University in Pittsburgh and the University of Detroit Mercy in Detroit, who have contributed ideas, topics for discussion, and challenges. To all of them, my infinite thanks and appreciation.

Table of Contents

Extended Table of Contents

Part I

Business and Strategy

Chapter 1

Technology in the Strategy of Organizations

"Without competitors, there would be no need for strategy, for the sole purpose of strategic planning is to enable the company to gain, as efficiently as possible, a sustainable edge over its competitors."

Kenichi Ohmae, "The Mind of The Strategist: The Art of Japanese Business" 1991.

1.1.- Learning objectives

- Understand the value of technology in organizations.
- Identify competitive strategies.
- Know the model of competitive forces and how technology can influence these forces.
- Define strategic management of information technologies.
- Appreciate the importance of the strategic management of information technologies.

1.2.- The emergence of strategic management of information systems

Not so long ago... there were no computers, smartphones, or the Internet. No one had those technologies. Telephones did not move and were connected to wires; answers came from encyclopedias printed in books and stored in buildings called libraries. People resorted to the radio or television to learn about the latest news. If someone wanted to announce a marriage or the birth of a child, the custom was to pay for a space in the local newspaper to share the happy occasion.

Suddenly, computer equipment began to appear among large companies. They did not do many things, nor were they used by ordinary people, but they saved time and money on certain repetitive activities.

As computers became more common and accessible, companies began to see that technology could save so much money that it was affordable and convenient to acquire and take advantage of their capabilities. New areas were created in the organization to manage this equipment, and experts in electronics and mathematics were hired to operate these computers.

It soon became apparent that just automating processes was no longer enough. Computers could be used to differentiate a company from its competitors. They could represent a competitive advantage and even modify the balance of forces in the marketplace.

At that moment, the world changed. If technology could reshape a product's market, decisions about what to do with the technology had to be overseen by tech-savvy business experts or tech experts with business knowledge. Creating new rules and principles was necessary to operate these innovations in that context. The strategic management of information technologies was born.

1.3.- The value of technology for companies

One way to appreciate how much value technology brings to organizations is by analyzing how much money companies are willing to pay for technological advances. If technology is important, customers will be ready to pay for it, and technology provider companies' market value should be high.

An accepted measure of the value of a company is by calculating its market capitalization, that is, the value that would be obtained if all the company shares were sold at the current market price. This number is very dynamic. Stock prices constantly vary, but as of January 2023, five of the ten companies with the highest market capitalization in the world were engaged in technology. Table 1.1 shows the list.

Table 1.1.– The companies with the highest market capitalization in January 2023. Source: Companiesmarketcap.com

Rank	Name	Market Cap	Price	Country
1	Apple	$1.989 T	$ 125.07	USA
2	Saudi Aramco	$1.887 T	$ 8.58	S. Arabia
3	Microsoft	$1.785 T	$ 239.58	USA
4	Alphabet (Google)	$1.157 T	$ 89.70	USA
5	Amazon	$875.5 B	$ 85.82	USA
6	Berkshire Hathaway	$684.14 B	$ 309.91	USA
7	United Health	$484.59 B	$ 518.64	USA
8	Johnson & Johnson	$465.87 B	$ 178.19	USA
9	Visa	$439.17 B	$ 207.39	USA
10	Exxon Mobil	$438.63 B	$ 106.51	USA

Similarly, when consulting the list of the wealthiest people on the planet, we find that seven of the ten richest people in the world made their fortune in technology. Table 1.2 shows the list according to Forbes magazine in January 2023.

Table 1.2.- List of the wealthiest people in the world in January 2023. Source: Forbes - [Dolan & Peterson-Withorn, 2023]

Rank	Name	Net Worth	Country	Source	Industry
1	Elon Musk	$219 B	USA	Tesla, SpaceX	Automotive & Technology
2	Jeff Bezos	$171 B	USA	Amazon	Technology
3	Bernard Arnault & family	$158 B	France	LVMH	Fashion & Retail
4	Bill Gates	$129 B	USA	Microsoft	Technology
5	Warren Buffett	$118 B	USA	Berkshire Hathaway	Finance & Investments
6	Larry Page	$111 B	USA	Google	Technology
7	Sergey Brin	$107 B	USA	Google	Technology
8	Larry Ellison	$106 B	USA	software	Technology
9	Steve Ballmer	$91.4 B	USA	Microsoft	Technology
10	Mukesh Ambani	$90.7 B	India	diversified	Diversified

1.4.- Competitive strategies

A strategy is how a company tries to differentiate itself from its competitors, using its corporate strengths to meet its customers' needs [Ohmae, 1991]. There are three generic competitive strategies:

1. Low prices
2. Differentiation
3. Niche market

Using the strategy of low prices, a company seeks to make its products cheaper than its competitors. Lower prices attract customers. The problem with this strategy is that if production and operating costs are relatively fixed, reducing the selling price of the same number of products would reduce revenues and profits. This strategy works if the company can produce and sell large quantities of products while maintaining a reasonable cost. The profits become significant if you earn little with each sale but sell a lot.

The differentiation strategy consists of changing something in the product, be it the packaging, the size, the way it is delivered, etc. That change can make the product feel different from its competitors. In that case, the price is not critical. Customers can pay more for similar products if one arrives at the right time or in a more convenient package. Examples would be first-class vs. economy-class seats on a commercial flight. All passengers travel on the same plane, at the same time, and on the same route. Everyone receives the same final product (getting to their destination), but first-class passengers pay much more for a ticket. The difference is in the service they receive on board the plane. For many, that difference makes the extra cost worthwhile.

The niche market strategy involves identifying customers obliged to buy our product. That is, they have no choice. If that is the case, the price is not a significant concern, and the product can be sold at a higher price than on the open market. For example, a drink in a football stadium during a game costs much more than the same drink bought in a supermarket, but the fan does not have the option to leave the stadium to buy drinks elsewhere.

Mini-case: Same seat, two different prices

Many airlines provide different classes of service on the same flights. A first-class ticket can cost three or up to five times more than a ticket on the same economy class flight. It's easy to see why people can accept this difference: there are bigger seats, better services on board, and you get on and off the plane a little faster.

Few people can appreciate that in the economy class cabin, passengers may be paying very different prices for the same seat and level of service.

Automatic reservation systems adjust the price of each ticket based on the supply and demand for spaces on that route and the other components of a customer's trip.

A passenger traveling from Monterrey to Dallas within two weeks in economy class would pay $800, while if the flight is in a month, the price would be $319.

Similarly, if someone wants to take a flight from Monterrey to Miami in two weeks and makes a stopover in Dallas, they would pay for a seat on the plane to Dallas plus a seat on the plane from Dallas to Miami, a total of $ 752. The total price is less than if you only used one seat on the flight to Dallas.

Two people traveling on the same route, at the same time, and on the same level of service may be paying very different prices for their seats.

Price source: Expedia.com

1.5.- Defining competition

Traditionally, a company's strength was measured by the growth of its market and the percentage of that market it owned. However, everything changed when Prof. Michael Porter clarified that several forces affect markets and that managing them can differentiate the company or change the rules of the competition in an entire market [Porter and Millard, 1985].

Porter found five forces that can influence the power of a company, which he called the competitive forces model. Market power is not only measured by the rivalry between current competitors but also by the possibility that a new competitor will enter the market that changes the balance of power with customers or that a substitute product will appear, making people stop buying ours. Getting close to the customer or having better bargaining power with suppliers can also affect competitiveness.

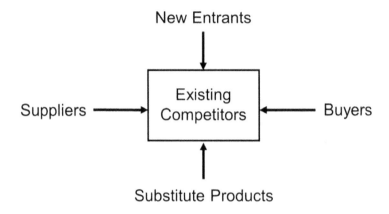

Figure 1.1.- Elements of Porter's Competitive Forces Model [Porter 1980]

1.6.- The role of information technology in competitiveness

As soon as Porter published his model of competitive forces, it became clear that there were instances where information technology could help a company get closer to its customers or suppliers or block new entrants or substitute products. For example, American Airlines built an airline ticket reservation system that allowed a travel agent to see all available flights and fares between two points identifying different flight plans for a customer. The reservation system changed the relationship between the airline and the travel agencies giving American Airlines an advantage. Additionally, given the level of investment required to build such a system, it was difficult for new competitors to enter that market unless they had substantial resources. In this case, a new technology gave American Airlines a competitive advantage.

> **Mini-case: The global wristwatch market**
>
> Swiss watches have been recognized worldwide for their precision and quality for many years. Having a Swiss watch was a status symbol. Consumers appreciated brands such as Swatch, Tissot, TAG Heuer, and Omega. Some people equate a Swiss watch with a prized jewel, as with watches from Rolex or Patek Philippe.
>
> The Swiss watch industry has been hit from different fronts: cheap watches produced in the East, digital watches, and even cell phones compete in some way with Swiss wristwatches. One of the most significant attacks began in September 2014 when Apple announced the iWatch, a wristwatch that also connects to the phone and allows access to countless functions.
>
> The iWatch had such a level of acceptance that in 2019 Apple sold 30.7 million watches, much more than the 21.1 million watches sold by all Swiss brands combined.
>
> Source: [Kharpal, 2020; Montredo, 2019; Apple Insider, 2023]

Warren McFarlan [1984] published a list of questions to ask in an industry to identify whether technology can provide a competitive advantage:

- Can technology change the balance of power between the company and its customers or suppliers?
- Can technology create barriers that make it harder to enter the market?
- Can technology reduce production costs or change the rules of competition?

If the answer to any of these questions is yes, then technology has the potential to become a tool of competitiveness, and the decision to adopt it is not technical; it is a strategic decision. Technology is no longer purely operational. It is a matter of high-level strategy. The question is: is the company ready to change the rules of the market and come out ahead?

The most dramatic market changes occurred with the birth of e-commerce. Companies such as Airbnb, Uber, Amazon, and Netflix changed the balance of power in their markets. They caused traditional competitors to face new challenges and even closed by not being able to compete under the new rules.

Mini-case: "And tune in next week at the same time for another episode of...."

At the dawn of the televised series, it was almost necessary to hear the phrase, "don't miss our next episode..." People tuned in to TV stations, week after week, at the same time, to watch a new episode of their favorite shows.

Today it is difficult to find series on free-access television channels, and it is more difficult to find someone willing to wait a week to see the next episode. We are used to "marathoning" the series; people watch all sixteen episodes of the show's first season on a single weekend.

These changes in the market were made possible by technologies such as streaming and content companies such as Netflix, Amazon Prime Video, HBO Go, or Clear video.

Source: Avast, Selectra [2023]

1.7.- Components of technological solutions

When talking about technology, many people think of computer equipment. However, the broader definition of information technology combines the architectures, tools, databases, analytical tools, applications, and methodologies necessary to make decisions and operate an organization. This definition is consistent with the classical views, which state that:

An information system is an integrated user-machine system for providing information that supports operations, management, and decision-making functions in an organization. The system uses computer equipment and software; manual procedures; models for analysis, planning, control, and decision-making; and a database. [Davis & Olson, 1985].

Separating the definition, we find that:

An information system is:

- An integrated user-machine system
- To provide information
- Supports operations, management, and decision-making functions
- In an organization

The system uses:

- Computer equipment and software
- Manual procedures
- Models for analysis, planning, control, and decision making
- A database

An information system is not a single component; it is an integrated system. Data is received from many sources, and different areas are involved. User-machine means that the system produces information for people, and people are involved in the process.

The goal of an information system is to support the functions and decisions of the organization. Most companies do not aim to have information systems. They use them because it helps them operate, manage, or make better decisions. Therefore, information systems help companies meet their goals.

The second part of the definition talks about the components. A computer (hardware) alone is useless. An information system needs programs (software) to operate. But the system is not just the computer and computer programs. It also requires manual procedures before, during, and after processing. Figure 1.1 illustrates the components of an information system.

This definition shows that, from the functional point of view, three basic subsystems are appreciated: the data subsystem, the analysis subsystem, and the user. The first element gathers and prepares data from different sources. The second element processes the data converting it into useful information that is received by the third component, the user, who is the one who takes advantage of the results to generate value for the organization.

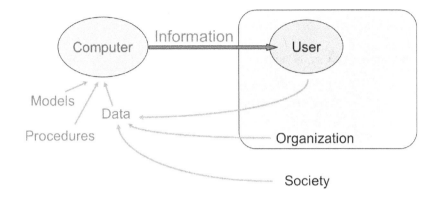

Figure 1.2.- Components of an information system

The information required to make decisions, operate, and manage a company comes from external sources and sources internal to the organization. A company has no single information system to get all the data. In reality, the data comes from several different elements. Computers can help in the company's operation, inventory management, sales, administrative control, and even the business's accounting. Operational excellence is often achieved using independent systems, a data source for business decisions.

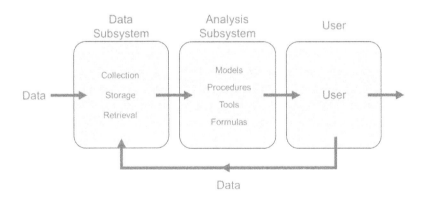

Figure 1.3.- Functional components of a business intelligence system

1.8.- Strategic management of information technology

The strategic management of information technologies consists of the architectures, tools, databases, analytical tools, applications, and methodologies necessary for the company to achieve its goals and remain competitive in a changing and globalized market.

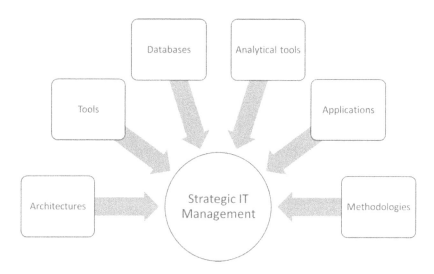

Figure 1.4.- Disciplines involved with the strategic planning of technologies

Defining the elements necessary for the company to achieve its goals and remain competitive in a changing and globalized market requires knowledge of information technologies and business, as well as an understanding of how to organize, operate and adapt the technologies available in the company.

The objective of this book is: to discuss techniques, standards, and best practices for managing information technology elements and processes in the organization; analyze the value that technology provides to the company, and discuss some additional abilities required of the persons responsible for managing the technology area.

The book is divided into five modules. The first discusses technology's value in business strategy. The second module focuses on leveraging technology in the enterprise and delivering the value investors expect. Module three focuses on how an area of information technology is operated in an organization. The fourth module discusses the delivery of services, components, and the relationship with technology providers. Finally, module five addresses some critical skills that the persons responsible for managing the technology area in the company must possess, in addition to their technological and administrative skills.

1.9.- Summary

- When technology started reshaping a product's market, it became necessary to create new rules and principles to operate these innovations. The strategic management of information technologies was born.
- There are three generic competitive strategies: low prices, differentiation, and niche markets.
- The competitive forces model indicates that market power is not only measured by the rivalry between current competitors but also by the possibility of a new competitor, a substitute product, or a change in the balance of power with customers or suppliers entering the market.
- If technology can influence competitive forces, then it has the potential to become a tool for competitiveness.
- The strategic management of information technologies consists of the architectures, tools, databases, analytical tools, applications, and methodologies necessary for the company to achieve its goals and remain competitive in a changing and globalized market.

1.10.- Review exercises

Questions

1. Define strategic management of information technologies.
2. Why is the market value of tech companies so high?
3. What are the three generic competitive strategies?
4. What are the five forces of the competitive forces model?
5. How can we know in a market if technology can be considered a tool to compete?
6. What is an information system?
7. What are the disciplines involved with strategic technology planning?

Exercises

1. Find an up-to-date list of companies with the largest market capitalization. What changed against the list in the book? Why?
2. Find an up-to-date list of the wealthiest people in the world. What changed against the list in the book? Why?
3. Identify a company that competes using low prices, another that competes by differentiation, and a third that uses niche markets as a strategy.
4. List two companies that offer similar products but at different prices. Why is there such a difference?
5. Identify and explain the effect of the Internet on the competitive forces in the retail market.
6. Find a market that has changed because of technology other than the Internet.

Chapter 2

Tools for Strategic IT Management

"I set high but not impossible standards. Mine are achievable with maximum effort."

Colin Powell, It Worked for Me, 2012.

2.1.- Learning objectives

- Understand the elements that define the business strategy.
- Identify the components of strategic management and how the balanced scorecard can support them.
- Recognize the value of strategic execution and understand the activities that define it.
- Know what quality management is and what role the ISO 9001:2015 standard plays in this process.
- Understand the corporate governance of TI and how the COBIT standard helps in its creation.
- Identify an IT area's deliverables and technological support and the role of ITIL in their specification.
- Recognize the stages of the IT implementation process and the value of CMMI in this process.

2.2.- Areas of the company relevant to the strategic management of technology

As mentioned in the previous chapter, strategic management of information technologies consists of the definition of the architectures, tools, databases, analytical tools, applications, and methodologies necessary for the company to achieve its goals and remain competitive in a changing and globalized market.

The objective of technology planning is not to have attractive technologies, nor is it even to have the latest technologies. The goal is to have the necessary technologies for the company to achieve its goals.

Therefore, it is crucial to understand the elements that define the business strategy before defining the technological strategy. Figure 2.1 describes the areas of company management that are relevant to the definition of the technology strategy.

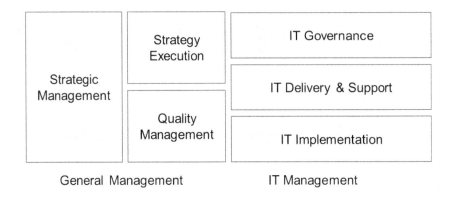

Figure 2.1.- Areas of company administration that are relevant to the definition of technology strategy [Lankhorst et al., 2009]

From figure 2.1, it is clear that there are areas of general administration that influence the functions and objectives of the areas of technology management: Strategic management, whose aim is to define the direction that the company must follow and its competitive strategy; Strategy execution, which focuses on how business strategies are put in place; and Quality Management, which consists of the activities that must be carried out to maintain the levels of excellence desired by the company.

Additionally, technology management can be classified into three areas that can generally be organized into IT governance, which defines the organizational and leadership structures that ensure that the company's IT resources can maintain and extend its strategic objectives. Deliverables and technological support determine the products that the technology area must deliver to support the operations and plans of the company, and IT Implementation, which focuses on the strategies for creating the technological solutions necessary for the organization.

2.3.- Strategic management

Strategic management defines the direction that the company must follow and its competitive strategy. Answer the questions What should I do? and Why is it important?

Strategic management is a topic that has been covered in business books for many years. Depending on who is consulted, there may be different formal definitions of what it means.

In trying to define strategic management, Nag, Hambrig, and Chen [2007] analyzed the publications of 57 authors and organized their ideas by field of work. They found three formal definitions of strategic management from the management point of view:

- "Developing an explanation of firm performance by understanding the roles of external and internal environments, positioning and managing within these environments and relating competencies and advantages to opportunities within external environments."
- "Strategic management is the process of building capabilities that allow a firm to create value for customers, shareholders, and society while operating in competitive markets."
- "The study of decisions and actions taken by top executives/TMTs for firms to be competitive in the marketplace."

Michael Porter [1980] defines strategy as the general formula of how a business will compete, its objectives, and the policies necessary to achieve those objectives. It speaks of the goals and the means required to achieve them. Additionally, it indicates that the strategy relates a company to its environment.

A tool to support organizations in formulating their strategy is the Balanced Score Card created by Robert Kaplan and David Norton [Kaplan & Norton, 1992]. The tool allows structuring the strategic objectives dynamically and integrally to test them according to a series of indicators that evaluate the performance of all the initiatives and projects necessary to achieve satisfactory compliance [Roncancio, 2018].

Traditionally, companies based their strategic models only on economic indicators. Kaplan and Norton explain that this vision is insufficient and argue that it should be supplemented by measuring customer satisfaction, internal processes, and the ability to innovate.

The tool focuses on the company from four perspectives. The first is the customer perspective, which measures how the company should present itself to customers using indicators such as customer satisfaction. The second perspective is financial and focuses on the value created by the company by measuring shareholder value. The internal business process perspective focuses on the effectiveness and efficiency of the company's internal processes. Finally, the learning and growth perspective measures the ability of the company and individuals to change and improve.

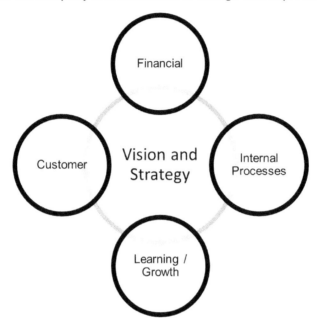

Figure 2.2.- Four perspectives of the Balanced Score Card

2.4.- Strategy execution

Strategy execution focuses on how business strategies are put in place. In a way, it answers the question: How will I do it?

Typically when asking for a definition of strategy execution, people say it's the correct implementation of a business plan or making sure the strategy is executed. But to understand the execution requires knowing the activities that it implies.

The American Management Association lists ten activities that define strategy execution [Barrows, 2019]:

1 - Visualize the strategy: Sometimes, it helps to put the plan's elements on a graph and illustrate how they interrelate. Frameworks such as Kaplan and Norton's Strategy Map [2004], Michael Porter's Activity Map [1996], or

Andy Neely's Success Map [Neely, Adams, and Crowe, 2001] can help in the visualization efforts

2 – Measure the strategy: Define the performance measurements in a balanced scorecard

3 – Report progress: just as the budget is monitored monthly, strategy measurements should be analyzed to see if the expected results are being obtained

4 – Make decisions: it is crucial to keep an eye on the environment and correct the course if conditions have changed.

5 – Identify strategy projects: An organization can have hundreds of projects. The first step is to list and organize all projects, particularly those with the most significant interference in the strategy.

6 – Align projects and strategy: Once projects have been identified, they must be aligned with the organization's strategy. Only those projects that support some organizational goal should receive funding and continue.

7 – Manage projects: it is vital to develop project management skills to secure effective execution.

8 – Communicate the strategy: The strategy should be communicated to all staff so they know what should be done and why it is essential.

9 – Align individual roles: Employees must understand how their role contributes to achieving the organization's objectives.

10 – Reward performance: The phrase "what is measured is improved" can be expanded to "what is measured and rewarded is improved faster."

2.5.- Quality management

Quality management consists of the activities that must be carried out to maintain the levels of excellence desired by the company. The question at this point is not what to do but how to make sure it is done well.

A standard that describes the criteria for good quality management is ISO 9001. The tool applies to any company size and field of activity [ISO, 2023]. The principle of quality is to ensure that the processes are well defined and documented and that the company's personnel know and follow those processes so that the results are the same each time they are executed. Additionally, there must be a mechanism for continuous improvement. This way, consistent results are always ensured, eventually generating quality results.

ISO 9001 revolves around Deming's four quality improvement steps [ASQ, 2023]: Plan, Do, Check, Act. Planning focuses on defining the objectives and processes necessary to meet the goals. Doing is implementing those processes. Verify measures the results of executed operations. Acting takes action to correct divergences and continuously improve the performance of operations.

Figure 2.3.- PDCA Cycle

The most recent version of the standard is called ISO 9001:2015 and consists of ten main clauses [Smart Business, 2017]

    0. Introduction
    1. Scope
    2. Normative reference
    3. Terms and definitions
    4. Context of the organization
    5. Leadership
    6. Planning
    7. Support
    8. Operation
    9. Performance evaluation
    10. Improvement

Figure 2.4 shows the relationship between the clauses of ISO 9001:2015 and the phases of the PDCA cycle.

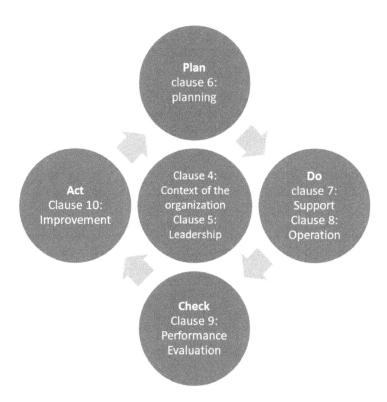

Figure 2.4.- Relationship between the clauses of ISO 9001:2015 and the
PDCA cycle [Source: 9001Academy, 2023]

2.6.- IT governance

IT governance consists of the organizational and leadership structures that ensure that the company's IT resources can maintain and extend its strategic objectives. It defines what needs to be achieved with information technology and how.

Another definition of IT governance comes from Peter Weill [2004], who defines it as "... specify frameworks for decision and liability rights that promote desirable behavior in the use of IT."

Combining both definitions: IT governance consists of the organizational structures and processes that ensure that IT functions to support and extend the organization's strategic objectives, promoting the best use of technologies for the company's purposes.

An international standard to help companies develop, organize and implement strategies around IT governance is COBIT (Control Objectives for Information and Related Technologies), a standard developed by ISACA in use around the world [White, 2019].

COBIT defines a series of generic processes that can serve as a reference model for IT management. For each resource, it defines its inputs, outputs, key activities, process objectives, performance measures, and a basic maturity model [ISACA, 2023]

The standard defines 34 processes covering 210 control objectives, classified into four domains:

1. Planning and Organization
2. Acquisition and Implementation
3. Delivery & Support
4. Monitoring and Evaluation

2.7.- IT delivery and support

Deliverables and technology support define the products the IT area must deliver to support the company's operations and plans. Answer the question What should I do?

Once the organization's processes have been defined, the technology area must identify the services and support that these processes require. One tool that describes best practices in IT service delivery is ITIL (Information Technology Infrastructure Library) [Hanna et al., 2009]

ITIL comprises a series of documents that guide the delivery of good IT services and the facilities necessary to support these services. The tool provides organizations with procedures to help them organize and manage the quality of services and technological infrastructure.

The foundation of ITIL focuses on two groups of processes:

- **Service delivery:** comprised of service level management, availability management, IT service financial management, IT contingency management, and capacity management
- **Service support:** covering problem management, incident management, help desk, change management, version management, and configuration management.

In 2019 ITIL V4 was introduced. It presents the value chain of the service consisting of six stages [Anand 2019]:

- **Engage**: Interact with external stakeholders to foster good understanding.
- **Plan**: Understand the vision, status, and directions for improvement of products and services.
- **Improve**: Ensure the continuous improvement of products, services, and practices throughout the value chain.
- **Design and transition**: Ensure that products and services consistently meet quality, cost, and time to market expectations.
- **Obtain / Build**: Ensure that products and services are available when and where they are needed, meeting specifications.
- **Deliver and support**: Ensure that products and services are delivered and supported to specifications.

ITIL complements COBIT. So COBIT control objectives are implemented using ITIL [Lankhorst et al., 2009].

2.8.- IT implementation

IT implementation focuses on strategies for creating the technological solutions necessary for the organization. The aim is to make sure systems are built correctly.

Several tools and methodologies exist for systems analysis, design, and software engineering. One of the standards most widely used for managing software development processes is CMM (Capability Maturity Model) and CMMI (Capability Maturity Model Integration) [Humphrey, 1988].

The CMMI maturation model consists of five levels:

CMMI 1 – Initial – The company does not have a stable software development environment. Processes are generally ad hoc and chaotic

CMMI 2 – Managed – The company has some general project management practices. Processes are managed, measured, and controlled. However, every project is different

CMMI 3 – Defined – Organizations have good project management, group coordination procedures, staff training, and better process metrics. There is consistency in the organization.

CMMI 4 – Quantitatively Managed – Focuses on quality and productivity metrics for risk management and decision making. The software produced is of high quality.

CMMI 5 – Optimizing – Process performance is constantly improved through incremental improvements and technological innovations. Metrics are used intensively, and the innovation process is managed.

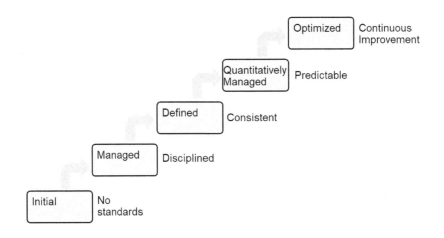

Figure 2.5.- CMMI maturation levels

2.9.- Summary

- Defining technology strategy requires understanding an organization's general and technology management needs.
- Areas of general management include strategic management, strategy execution, and quality management. Technology management includes IT governance, IT deliverables and support, and IT implementation
- Strategic management defines the direction that the company must follow and its competitive strategy. Determines what should be done and why it is essential. A tool to support organizations in formulating their strategy is the Balanced Score Card
- Strategy execution focuses on how business strategies are put in place. In a way, it defines how the company works.
- Quality management consists of the activities that must be carried out to maintain the levels of excellence desired by the company. At

this point, the objective is to do things right. A standard that describes the criteria for good quality management is ISO 9001.

- IT governance consists of the organizational and leadership structures that ensure that the company's IT resources can maintain and extend its strategic objectives. Answer the question of what do I want to achieve? And why? An international standard to help companies develop, organize and implement strategies around IT governance is COBIT (Control Objectives for Information and Related Technologies).

- Deliverables and Technology Support defines the products that IT must deliver to support the company's operations and plans. Answer the question What should I do? One tool that describes best practices in IT service delivery is ITIL (Information Technology Infrastructure Library).

- IT implementation focuses on strategies for creating the technological solutions necessary for the organization. One of the most used standards for managing software development processes is CMM (Capability Maturity Model) and a CMMI (Capability Maturity Model Integration) extension.

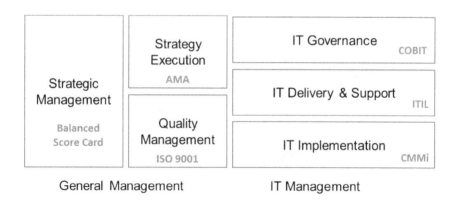

Figure 2.6.- Standards of support for strategic activities [Lankhorst et al., 2009]

2.10.- Exercises

Questions

1. What is strategic management?
2. Why is it said that the Balanced Score Card can help strategic management?
3. How is strategic execution performed?
4. What are the ten activities that define the execution of the strategy according to the American Management Association?
5. What kind of company can use ISO 9001?
6. What is IT governance?
7. How can the COBIT standard help in IT governance?
8. What is the service value chain?
9. How does the CMMI standard support systems development?

Exercises

1. Find three companies that show to be ISO 9001 certified.
2. Look for a case showing the value of using COBIT in defining a company's IT policies.
3. Investigate how the ITIL standard has evolved.
4. Find out where to look for certification in ITIL.
5. Investigate how to get a CMMI certification.

Chapter 3

Enterprise Architecture Modeling

"Only among those who were engaged in a particular activity did their language remain unchanged; so, for instance, there was one for all the architects, one for all the carriers of stones, one for all the stone-breakers, and so on for all the different operations. As many as were the types of work involved in the enterprise, so many were the languages by which the human race was fragmented; and the more skill required for the type of work, the more rudimentary and barbaric the language they now spoke."

Dante Alighieri, (on the Tower of Babel), "De vulgari eloquentia", Chapter VII, 1305.

3.1.- Learning objectives

- Define enterprise architecture.
- Understand the relationship between the different levels of architecture in an organization.
- Learn the basic principles of process modeling using BPMN.
- Learn the basic principles of data modeling using entity-relationship diagrams.

3.2.- The importance of enterprise architecture modeling

It is agreed that the objective of information technologies is to support the company and help it meet its goals. Therefore, the first step to defining a technological strategy must be understanding the business strategy well. At this point, communication is essential. Generally, although corporate strategy can be summarized in mission or vision statements defined in a few words, these missions are achieved through complex mechanisms involving numerous employees developing countless tasks in different departments.

"An enterprise architecture is a blueprint of the structure, arrangement, configuration, functional groupings/partitioning, interfaces, data, protocols, logical functionality, integration, technology, of IT resources needed to support a corporate or organizational business function or mission. Typically, resources that need architectural formulations include applications, security subsystems, data structures, networks, hardware platforms, storage, and desktop systems, to name just a few" [Minoli, 2008].

The ANSI/IEEE standard states that architecture is "the fundamental organization of a system, embodied in its components, their relationships to each other and the environment, and the principles governing its design and evolution."

An analogy can be drawn between enterprise architecture and a map of a city. To understand the city, instead of walking all the streets, sometimes it is better to see it on a map. A map can show the roads, the buildings, and, if the map is interactive, even the traffic and time to reach a destination.

However, maps of a city can include much more than streets. Public transport routes, electrical wires, and gas pipes, among others, can also be represented. The requested blueprint will depend on the need for information, but all describe the city as a whole. Additionally, to be understood, different visions require different languages. Thus, electrical blueprints do not bear the same symbols as those for water pipes or other utilities.

Similarly, enterprise architecture has several perspectives and levels represented by different languages. These perspectives are discussed in the following sections.

3.3.- Levels of enterprise architecture

The first step in analyzing a company's enterprise architecture is looking at the organization's services. A service is a unit of functionality that some entity (a system, organization, or department) delivers to its environment and represents a value for another entity in the same domain. By following the source of the services needed for the company, you can understand the levels of abstraction required to map an organization.

When describing what a company does, its relationship with the customer represents the highest level of abstraction. In most cases, the customer receives the organization's products or services and represents its primary source of revenue. The customer can be someone other than an individual buying a product. Some companies provide services to other companies or raw materials that other organizations turn into products for their customers.

The customer receives the business services (referring to products or services per se). These services are the result of some business processes. So the highest layer in enterprise architecture is the customers who receive business services that are the product of business processes.

Each service layer provides a value to a top layer and is the product of a lower execution layer, which produces the service.

A business process consists of activities executed by entities (people or machines) that produce a good (product or service). Business processes need application services that are provided by applications or software systems. Therefore, the business process layer follows the application services layer that follows application components.

Each layer can be enlarged to show different sublevels. For example, an application consists of three main components, presentation services (the user interface), operation services (the algorithms and calculations), and data services (the information being handled).

An application needs infrastructure services that run on technological infrastructure or hardware. Figure 3.1 shows the architecture levels of an organization.

Each of these layers has its language and modeling method. Thus, modeling a business process uses a language different from the one used for modeling data or the hardware infrastructure of an organization.

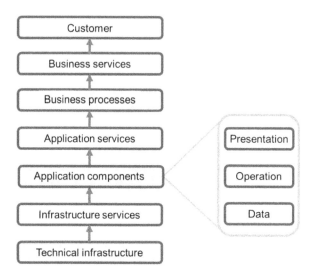

Figure 3.1.- Levels of the architecture of an organization (adapted from Lankhorst et al. [2019])

3.4.- Process modeling

There are several ways to understand how an organization works. If the organization looked like a machine and this machine had only one function and few parts, probably a glance would be all that would be required to understand it and know if the information it produces is accurate.

A simple analogy would be, in the physical world, what is known as a lever— a simple machine consisting of a rigid bar that can rotate around a fulcrum. The job of the lever is to transmit the force from one side of the lever to the other. Seeing it, a person would know that if pressure lowered the lever on one side, the other side would go up.

When words are not enough, a drawing can explain how the lever works. Figure 3.1 illustrates a lever and represents a simple machine.

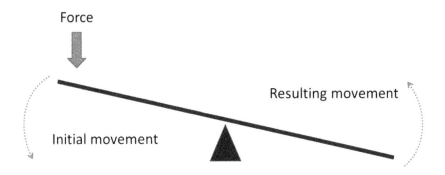

Figure 3.2.- illustration of a simple machine

A picture is worth a thousand words. Now imagine a complex machine, like the gasoline engine of a car. Understanding the workings and parts of an engine requires more than a single drawing. We would probably have to separate its functions and explain that while certain parts serve to start the engine, others make sure that it has the gasoline it needs to keep it running, while other parts focus on cooling it so that it does not stop working. In this case, the system (motor) would be composed of subsystems (starting, fuel, and cooling, among others).

> **Mini-case – How does an internal combustion engine work?**
>
> According to Wikipedia, "an internal combustion engine, explosion engine or piston engine is a type of machine that obtains mechanical energy directly from the chemical energy of a fuel that burns inside the combustion chamber... When the fuel mixed with oxygen in the engine burns, an explosion occurs that moves the piston causing the vehicle to advance." The engine consists of several subsystems: combustion chamber, power system, distribution system, ignition, cooling, and starting system. [Wikipedia, 2023]

Most organizations are complex entities with various activities and areas involved. Some activities include purchasing, sales, production, human resources, customer service, etc. Sometimes an area engages in multiple types of work. Such as the cashier of a convenience store, who receives money as payment for products but also receives cash deposits to bank accounts, pays debit card withdrawals, tops up transport cards, and delivers money sent by other people from other branches to a particular recipient. Other times, the participation of different areas is required to complete an activity. For example, when an employee asks for vacation, it usually requires authorization from the human resources area and their immediate boss.

There are several definitions of business process:

"A series of activities developed within an organization to achieve a business goal" [Weske, 2012]

"A set of functions, in a specific sequence, that in the end delivers value for an internal or external customer" [Kirchmer, 2017]

"A sequence of business activities that use resources to transform specific inputs into specific outputs to achieve a business goal" [Richardson, Chang & Smith, 2020]

It can be said that a **business process** is a series of activities, in a specific sequence, developed within an organization that uses resources to transform inputs into outputs, which they deliver to an internal or external customer, to achieve a business objective.

A company has several business processes interacting with entities outside the company (customers or other companies) by exchanging information or materials or with other internal processes or entities.

Each process can have sub-processes. Figures 3.3 and 3.4 illustrate a process and the detailed analysis of one of its functions or sub-processes.

Figure 3.3.- Simple business model

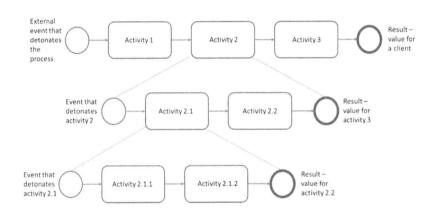

Figure 3.4.- Hierarchical decomposition of a process

Figures 3.3 and 3.4 used symbols to represent the processes and their components. These diagrams are known as **activity models**. There are different languages or standards for modeling activities in the organization. In this case, the figures are generated using the Business Process Model and Notation (BPMN) standard. Among the most commonly used notations in the industry for modeling processes are:

- Flowcharts
- Data Flow Diagrams (DFDs)
- Business Process Maps
- Business Process Model and Notation (BPMN)

Modeling a process makes sense because it helps the user understand what the process produces, the resources it occupies, and how it transforms inputs into outputs. Comparing the value of outcomes against the cost of the resources required can help determine whether a process is cost-effective.

Other reasons for modeling processes can be: to facilitate audits, communicate instructions to the company, standardize information exchanges with customers or suppliers, or train the personnel involved.

Once a system is modeled, its economic and operational efficiency can be analyzed. A well-made model can help identify useless threads or bottlenecks in some jobs. This analysis makes it possible to modify processes (evolution) or radically change them (revolution).

3.5.- Process modeling using BPMN

Business Process Model and Notation (BPMN) is a graphical way of representing the activities of a business process. It focuses on identifying the sequence of operations and the messages that flow between them [Nextech, 2021]. BPMN was initially developed by the Business Process Management Initiative (BPMI) and is currently maintained by the Object Management Group (OMG).

"Business Process Model and Notation has become the de-facto standard for business processes diagrams. It is intended to be used directly by the stakeholders who design, manage, and realize business processes, but at the same time, be precise enough to allow BPMN diagrams to be translated into software process components. BPMN has an easy-to-use flowchart-like notation independent of any particular implementation environment. " [Object Management Group, 2023]

BPMN uses a small set of symbols to facilitate its use among stakeholders. The four basic categories of elements are:

Flow Objects: Events, Activities, Flow Control (gateways);

Connection Objects: Sequence Flow, Message Flow, Association;

Swim lanes: Pool, Lane;

Artifacts: Data Objects, Group, Annotation.

Flow objects

Flow objects represent the concepts being modeled. There are three types of objects:

Activities (what is done): Show processes such as preparing an invoice, charging for a product, or packing sales. Activities can be atomic or compounded from sub-processes (Figure 3.3). Sometimes you want to show that a process is repeated several times (until a condition is met). Some processes occur in parallel (such as when all students take the same exam), and sequential processes are repeated several times (such as when the teacher grades everyone's exams, one at a time).

Events: They describe something happening (usually out of the company's control). Events can initiate a process or receive its products. Examples of triggers would be a request for information or a sale. Examples of final events could be the receipt of a statement. The primary events are beginning, intermediate, and end. However, three types of additional events can also help describe processes. The first type is message events, which are communications between one participant and another, and serve to initiate a process or report progress. The second type is time events (or timers); these are used to indicate that some activity should start at a specific time (startup timer) or wait some time (intermediate timer). The third type is error events; they show an interruption in the process and usually trigger alternate activities to handle errors.

Flow controls: Indicate branches or junctions in the flow. They usually come in pairs; one flow control separates the flow into different alternatives, while another brings together the various paths at the end.

There are different types of flow controls: exclusive (only one alternative is possible), inclusive (you can opt for one or more paths), and parallel (you must travel all routes).

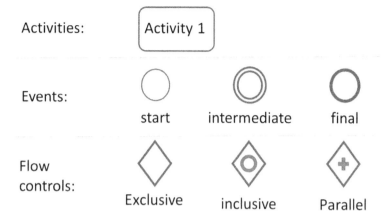

Activities:

Activity 1

Events:

start   intermediate   final

Flow controls:

Exclusive   inclusive   Parallel

Figure 3.5.- Flow objects

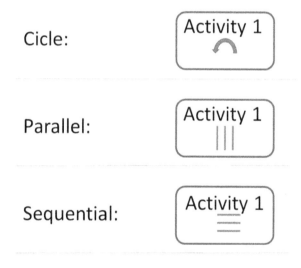

Cicle:

Activity 1

Parallel:

Activity 1

Sequential:

Activity 1

Figure 3.6.- Repetitive activities

Message:

receive   send

start   intermedate   end

Timer:

start   intermediate

Intermediate error:

Figure 3.7.- Types of events

Connection objects

Connection objects join flow objects. There are three types of connection objects:

Sequence **flows** show the order in which activities will be carried out. Indicates that one activity precedes, or follows, another.

Message **flows** connect internal processes with processes or entities (companies) outside ours.

Associations connect a text to a flow object

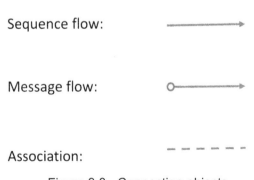

Sequence flow:

Message flow:

Association:

Figure 3.8.- Connection objects

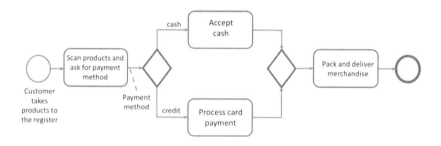

Figure 3.9.- Example of BPMN of the payment process in a supermarket

Swim lanes

BPMN represents organizations and departments grouping their functions into pools and swim lanes.

A **pool:** Represents a more significant participant, usually an entire company. Companies are separated into one or more departments, represented by swim lanes. A pool can be open, where it is possible to see their components, or closed, illustrated by boxes that only show the flows of information and materials from and to other organizations and not what happens inside the box.

A **lane:** Represents an activity, role, or process within an organization.

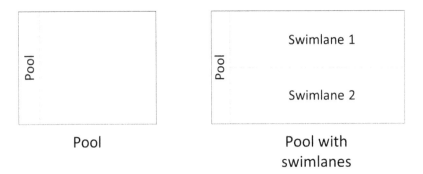

Pool   Pool with
                                        swimlanes

Figure 3.10.- Pools and swimming lanes

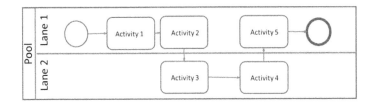

Figure 3.11.- Example of processes in swimming lanes

Artifacts: Data Objects, Group, Annotation.

Sometimes, additional information needs to be added so that the diagrams can be better understood. There are three primary artifacts: data objects, groups, and annotations.

Data **objects** show what data is produced or required by some process. For example, the credit card payment process would require the card number and expiration date, among others.

Groups visually bring together some activities without affecting their flow. They are represented with a dotted rectangle with rounded corners.

Annotations are used to give more information and make diagrams more understandable

Figure 3.12.- Artifacts

3.6.- Examples of process models

Appointment with a doctor

The patient calls the doctor's office and requests an appointment; the office offers available times; the patient chooses a time and date, and the reservation is made.

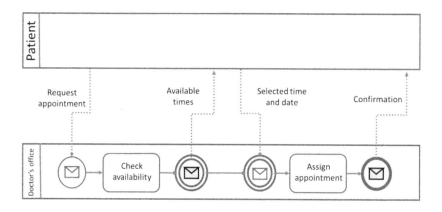

Figure 3.13.- Appointment with a doctor

Invitation to a concert

An invitation is presented to a person to attend a concert in one week. If the invitation is accepted, what is required is to wait a week and go to the show. If the invitation is rejected, it is automatically canceled.

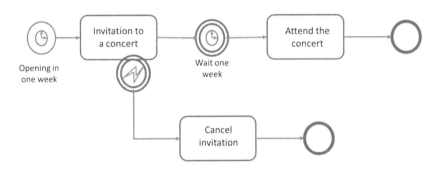

Figure 3.14.- An invitation to a concert that takes place in one week

Buy t-shirts in an online store

The customer requests one or more types of t-shirts from an online store. The store may or may not have the models and sizes in stock—the store requests from the manufacturer any missing t-shirts. The order is assembled. Once payment is received, the t-shirts are packed and delivered.

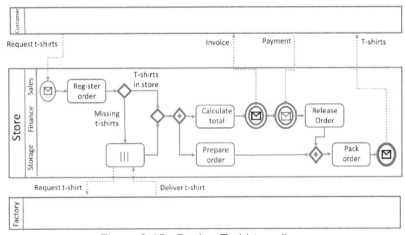

Figure 3.15.- Buying T-shirts online

3.7.- Tips for process modeling

Process modeling aims to communicate what a process does and how it does it. The diagram or the diagrams that result must be understandable by the person to whom they are addressed. The human mind can handle a limited amount of data before falling to the point of information overload. Each layer of a process map should be as simple as possible. If a process has too many components, consider grouping some functions into a single, more extensive operation and taking the detail to the next level, such as subprocesses of the macro process. Include the basics, but don't get lost in the details.

Divide complex processes into several small ones, and if the results are still too large, divide them again.

When modeling, focus on one process at a time.

When tagging activities, use a verb and a noun (for example: deliver orders, receive payments, calculate costs).

Go through the workflow and check that you did not forget anything. Be iterative, generate the first version, and correct it as you review the process.

Validate your diagrams with the people who are performing the processes. When they see what the figures say they do, they will know if something mentioned is inaccurate or if any conditions are missing.

3.8.- Data modeling

A data element is a representation of reality that describes a characteristic of an entity. Each entity can be represented by different data elements, depending on its complexity. For example, one person can have a name but also an address or an age.

Data models are abstract representations of data elements, their relationships, and the properties of the real-world entities represented by those elements.

Data models provide a vision of how records are made, how information is accumulated and related, what categories of data are used in each case, what characteristics they have (for example, length, restrictions, etc.), and what policies they have to comply.

A data model can be designed from different perspectives according to its use: diagramming the information from a **conceptual standpoint** (which indicates <u>what</u> the database contains); from a **logical perspective** (which details <u>how it should behave</u>, developing a map of rules and the characteristics of the structures, with their validations, exceptions, and relationships between values); or from a **physical Perspective** (showing <u>how it is implemented</u> in a way applied to the specific database, with the technical information of the tables and columns and the type of data used).

There are different ways of representing data in a model. Two popular modeling languages are the Unified Modeling Language (UML) Class Model and the Entity-Relationship Model (discussed below).

3.9.- Entity-Relationship Models (E-R)

An **Entity-Relationship Model** is a diagram that explains how a database is designed. The model shows the entities in the database, how they work together, and their attributes. The fundamental components of the E-R model are the entities, their characteristics, and the relationship between entities.

Entity refers to any object, being, or concept from which you want to collect data points. An entity contains some **attributes** or characteristics (such as name, age, salary, hours worked, etc.)

Identifying attributes or **key attributes** refer to a characteristic of an individual entity unique to that entity and differentiates it from other entities of the same class (say, the equivalent of a primary key, such as the customer number or ID, the item number, or even the username in the creation of an email).

Relationships tell us how entities associate (usually represented by verbs). Cardinalities (called "multiplicities" in UML) represent the ratio of entities on one side to entities on the other side of the relationship. They can be one-to-one, one-to-many, or many-to-many and are characterized by a pair of numbers identified at each end of the line showing the association.

In the Entity-Relationship Model, each of the related concepts is represented as follows:

- Entities: using a rectangle
- Attribute: using an oval/circle
- Relationship: employing a rhombus
- Cardinalities are defined by numbers next to the related entities and sometimes with these numbers above the relationship.

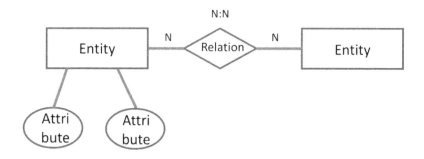

Figure 3.16.- Graphical Representation of Entity-Relationship Diagram

Below is an example of how an employee (entity) works (relationship) in a company (related entity) in an Entity-Relationship Model. In this example, many employees can work for the company. The connection is many to one (represented by the letter N and one at the linked ends by each entity). In this case, the information about an employee is their age and gender.

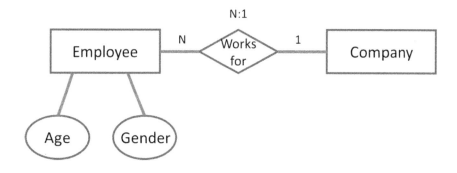

Figure 3.17.- Example of Entity-Relationship Diagram

Cardinality is represented with crow's foot notation

Sometimes cardinality is identified with symbology rather than the numbers on the sides of the entity. These symbols are depicted in how the line that connects the related entities ends on each side. Depending on the cardinality is how the connection finishes (see Figure 5.15), in many cases marking the minimums and maximums applicable for each end.

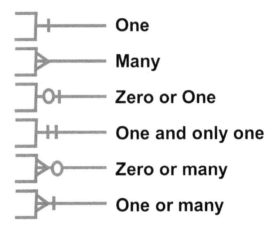

One

Many

Zero or One

One and only one

Zero or many

One or many

Figure 3.18.- Forms of representation of crow's foot notation

When the crow's foot notation is used, the rhombus of the relationship is not recorded. Linking both entities through the line with the fitting symbol at each end is enough.

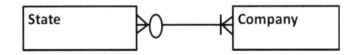

Figure 3.19.- Example of Entity-Relationship Diagram with crow's foot notation

In the example above, a company may have no employees or have several, represented by the left side of the line in the diagram. On the other hand, an employee can belong to a company or more simultaneously (for example, having two jobs), which is determined on the right side of the line.

The first step to converting an ER diagram into tables is to replace all the many to many relationships (N:N), creating intermediate entities with 1:N relationships.

For example, an invoice may include multiple items, and an item may appear on various invoices (representing an N:N ratio). Still, that relationship carries purchased units (an attribute), and the relationships have no attributes. To solve this and be able to translate the ER diagram into tables, we must first create an entity called the invoice line. The new entity contains only one item and appears in only one invoice, but the same item can be in several different invoice lines, and invoices can have many lines (see Figure 3.20).
The invoice line has as external keys the item number, the invoice number, as an internal key the line number, and as an attribute the number of items purchased on that line (which would calculate the total price).

Every entity becomes a table. Entities with 1:N relations include the key of the item to which they are linked as part of the table. The invoice line table consists of a column for invoice line number (as key), invoice number and item number (as foreign keys), and a column for units as its attribute.

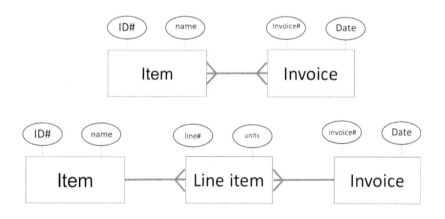

Figure 3.20.- Conversion of N:N ratios in E-R diagram to 1:N ratios for tables

Development of E-R Diagram in Purchase Orders in Candy Marketer

You own a store that buys and sells candies in bulk. You need purchase orders for your suppliers to operate the store. You need to know the supplier's name, the contact person's name, and email. For every item in the order, you need the description, price, and quantity to order.

To create an E-R diagram for the store's purchase orders, first, you must recognize as entities the supplier, the contact persons, the purchase order, and the products.

▫ A supplier may have several contacts, but a contact person works only for a single supplier (1:N ratio). Email is an attribute of the contact person.
▫ A purchase order may be related to a single supplier, but a supplier may be placed with different purchase orders (1:N ratio).
▫ A purchase order can have different types of sweets, one kind of candy can also be in other purchase orders, so the ratio is N:N).
▫ The description is an attribute of the candy. Quantity and price of the sweets are attributes of each purchase order's line. The date of generation and total amount are attributes of the purchase order.

Therefore, the relations between the parties would be in the first instance as follows:

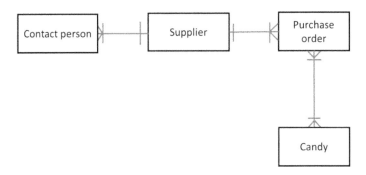

Figure 3.21.- Diagram E-R with the main relations for the purchase order

Derived from the relationship Many to Many that exists between Sweets and Purchase Order, to generate the table the above is divided as follows:

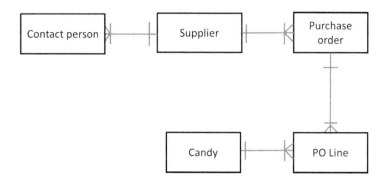

Figure 3.22.- Conversion to table of the relations for the purchase order

The above would be completed with the respective attributes in each case, according to the following Figure:

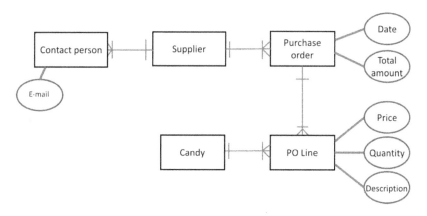

Figure 3.23.- Table of relations with attributes for the purchase order in a candy store

Mini-case – Data in a hat shop

Stephen's, an exclusive gentleman's hat shop, keeps track of all its customers. They know the buyer, model, size, and color of each hat sold. They also know when and how much was paid for each sale. The company also keeps track of the client's birthdays and, if applicable, the wives' birthdays.

Can you prepare an entity-relationship diagram showing the customer, hat, and purchase entities, with their relationships and attributes?

Mini-case – Registration data in a school

In a school that has semester programs, a teacher can teach different groups of different subjects every semester. Students can enroll in more than one course per semester. Not every course is offered each semester, but they can have more than one group when they are. A group can have several students registered but only one teacher.

How would this structure be represented in an entity-relationship diagram? What entities need to be modeled? What attributes does each entity have?

3.10.- Summary

- Enterprise architecture is a blueprint of the structure, arrangement, configuration, functional groupings/partitioning, interfaces, data, protocols, logical functionality, integration, and technology of IT resources needed to support a corporate or organizational business function or mission.
- The first step in analyzing a company's enterprise architecture is to look at the services the organization provides. A service is a unit of functionality that some entity (a system, organization, or department) delivers to its environment and represents a value for another entity in the same domain.

- When describing what a company does, the highest level is its relationship with the customer. Each service layer provides a value to a top layer and is the product of a lower execution layer, which produces the service. Each of these layers has its language and modeling method.
- A business process consists of activities executed by entities (people or machines) that produce a good (product or service). Business Process Model and Notation (BPMN) is a graphical way of representing the activities of a business process.
- Data models are abstract representations of data elements, their relationships, and the properties of the real-world entities represented by those elements. An Entity-Relationship Model is a diagram that explains how a database is designed—shows how entities in the database relate, including their attributes, and how they work together.

3.11.- Review exercises

Questions

1. What is the difference between describing a process and modeling it?
2. What is a business process?
3. It mentions the most commonly used notations in the industry to model processes.
4. What is BPMN?
5. What are the main flow objects in BPMN?
6. What is the difference between using a swim lane and a pool in BPMN notation?
7. What is a data model?
8. What is Unified Modeling Language (UML)?
9. What are the most significant benefits of using entity-relationship models?
10. What are the symbols used in entity-relationship diagrams?

Exercises

1. Prepare the diagram that describes how to order a taxi from an online service.
2. Describe the process a person follows in deciding which car to buy.
3. Visit a bank and analyze the process tellers follow to serve a customer. Prepare a BPMN model of those processes.
4. What are the steps required to request a copy of a birth certificate?

5. In an engine repair company, the procedure to pay for each job is as follows: A mechanic receives the engine with problems and records the start time of work. The first step is to check the faulty machine and diagnose the fault. The mechanic goes to the warehouse, requests the parts for the job, places them in the engine, and tests them. If there are extra unused parts, they return to the warehouse. If the fault persists and the mechanic needs more pieces, the mechanic prepares another order. At the end of the work, the mechanic records the ending time and declares the engine repaired. Calculating the total cost requires knowing the hours worked by the mechanic and the value of the parts used. Prepare an entity-relationship diagram where you show the mechanic, motor, spare parts, maintenance work, and spare parts used. Include all attributes and relationships. Make sure each entity has a primary key.

6. The organizing committee of a congress wants to keep its accounts clear. Each committee member receives a certain number of tickets that they must sell. Each ticket costs 10 dollars, but if a customer buys three, the price for the three tickets is 26 dollars. Packages of ten tickets sell for 70 dollars. As each member sells their tickets, they give the money to the treasurer, informing them how many they sold individually and how many packs of 3 and 10 tickets they have sold. Prepare an entity-relationship diagram that includes committee members, tickets given to each member, and single tickets (and packages of 3 and 10) sold by each member.

Part II

Governance

Chapter 4

IT Governance

"All members of the organization, in order to relate their efforts to the common good, must understand how their tasks fit in with the task of the whole. And, in turn, they must know what the task of the whole implies for their own tasks, their own contributions, their own directions."

Peter F. Drucker, "Management: Revised Edition," 2008

4.1.- Learning Objectives.

- Understand the principles of corporate governance.
- Know the differences between corporate governance and IT governance.
- Appreciate the importance for a company of having IT governance.
- Identify the roles involved with the definition and operation of IT governance.
- Understand the components of IT governance.
- Know the critical questions for each element of IT governance.

4.2.- What is corporate governance?

When people invest their money in a company, they expect that the organization's resources will be used in the best way to maximize the investor's profits and protect their assets. Typically, shareholders appoint a board of directors that looks after their interests, defines the company's objectives, and dictates the business's general rules of operation. The board sets the senior management that operates the company.

The Corporate Governance model is defined when the company's rules are created. Corporate governance focuses on the combination of processes and structures implemented by the board of directors to inform, direct, manage and monitor the organization's activities to achieve its objectives.

A more formal definition is: "Corporate governance is the system by which companies are directed and controlled. Boards of directors are responsible for the governance of their companies. The shareholders' role in governance is to appoint the directors and the auditors and to satisfy themselves that an appropriate governance structure is in place. The responsibilities of the board include setting the company's strategic aims, providing the leadership to put them into effect, supervising the management of the business, and reporting to shareholders on their stewardship. The board's actions are subject to laws, regulations, and the shareholders in general meeting." [Cadbury, 1992]

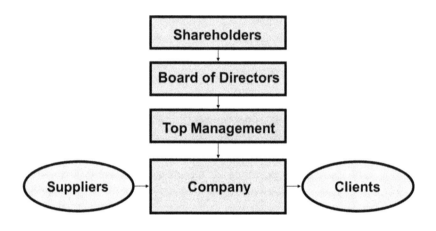

Figure 4.1.- Role of shareholders and top management in an organization

4.3.- What is IT governance?

In 1958, three years after the release of the first commercial computer, scientists identified a new phenomenon in organizations and called it "information technologies" [Leavitt & Whisler, 1958]. They predicted that by the mid to late 1980s (30 years later), these technologies would: allow senior executives to become more involved in the operation of the business, re-centralize activities, reduce the number of middle managers, and facilitate that fewer people could do more work.

Today it is common for organizations to invest in information and communication technologies. These technologies directly impact companies' results and allow them to reduce costs, increase sales, or even create new products. In some cases, the changes have been so radical that entire industries have changed the way they operate, causing the disappearance of traditional companies and the creation of new ones. Video rentals, taxis, hotels, and newspapers experienced radical changes.

Many companies had to rethink their business models: Kodak, after a hundred years of operation, had to refocus its activities; IBM sold its microcomputer division; Apple explored new markets like music and cellphones; Facebook serves more than one billion users in a type of business that did not exist only a few years ago.

A tool that can mean considerable profits for a company or change the basis of competition can put at risk the very existence of the business. It is the responsibility of senior management and the board of directors to ensure that this tool is handled in the best possible way to obtain profits and avoid losses.

Such is the effect of adequately managing IT resources in organizations that a study of 250 companies in 23 countries by Dr. Peter Weill, director of the Center for Information Research at MIT, found that, when comparing companies with similar strategic models, those that have superior IT governance models have been shown to make 20% more profit than counterparts who had poor models [Weill & Ross, 2004].

Technology is a critical asset, represents a significant expense, and can have vital strategic implications for the future of the business. The board of directors and senior management must ensure that the best results are obtained from their technology investments and that the company is well positioned to take advantage of the opportunities its markets offer without taking many risks.

According to the IT Governance Institute, an integral part of Corporate Governance is IT Governance. It consists of: "...the leadership and organizational structures and processes that ensure that the organization's IT function remains and extends the organization's strategic objectives."

Another definition of IT Governance comes from Peter Weill [2004], who defines it as "...Specifying the framework for decision rights and accountabilities to encourage desirable behavior in the use of IT."

Therefore, IT governance defines organizational structures and processes that ensure that IT supports and extends the organization's strategic objectives, promoting the best use of technologies for the company's purposes.

57

4.4.- Scope of IT Governance

Understanding the roles in defining and operating IT governance requires analyzing who benefits from these principles.

- **Investors, board of directors, and senior management:** Ensure that IT investments deliver optimal returns on their investments and compliance with laws and regulations.

- **Business unit managers:** Participate in strategic IT decisions, prioritize projects, and improve their performance and the predictability of their results.

- **Project managers:** Monitor their progress and can make decisions faster.

- **The IT area:** Facilitates the communication of how IT supports business objectives, helps prioritize its activities, and achieves greater coordination and collaboration with business units.

IT governance is the direct responsibility of the Board of Directors and senior management; however, as it is the operational responsibility of the CIO, and because this is the domain of their area of expertise, the CIO is directly responsible for the development and operation of the program. Additionally, the participation of those responsible for the business units is required. After all, they are the ones who understand the needs and opportunities of the business and the staff of the IT department because they will be responsible for its implementation.

Each role has a different level of involvement in the definition of IT governance. While the board of directors and senior management are responsible for writing and consulting the rules, other areas design and operate different components.

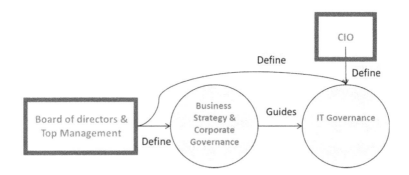

Figure 4.2.- Roles involved in defining IT governance

The following list of components of an IT governance strategy should help to understand the complexity of the decisions to be made and the importance of involving different areas.

The scope of IT governance includes:

- **IT principles:** A high-level view of the role IT plays in the enterprise.

- **IT architecture:** The definition of the equipment and platforms to be used, their location, and how they relate to each other, including the plan for their evolution, operation, and maintenance.

- **Application architecture:** The definition of information systems that solve business needs and how they interact with each other.

- **The service architecture:** Specify the response offered for the IT needs of the business areas and their users.

- **The investment and prioritization plan:** Defines how the resources allocated to IT will be invested.

- **The human resource development Plan:** Decisions on achieving and maintaining the technical and administrative skills needed to execute IT plans.

- **Policies, processes, tools, and techniques:** decisions regarding the tools to use and how to organize to take advantage of them.

The roles involved in the definition of IT governance and its components are:

- **The board of directors and senior management:** Define the business objectives, approve, monitor the IT plan, and direct investments in the area.

- **The Chief Information Officer (CIO):** assumes responsibility for preparing the plan and its components, including its operation and performance.

- **Business unit managers:** prepare requirements, approve and support IT projects, and define specifications and business objectives.

- **IT administrators:** assume responsibility for the development and operation of IT projects and the correct performance of technological solutions.

- **Technical staff:** are informed of the initiatives and their particular responsibilities.

4.5.- IT governance in action

IT governance answers three main questions that have to do with the meaning (strategy), management (execution), and measurement (value) of information technologies.

The questions that are answered are:

- Strategy: Are we doing the right things? What should we do?
- Execution: Are we doing them right?
- Value: Are we getting the benefits?

The steps to answer each question are:

Strategy (meaning):
- Aligning the IT plan with the business plan
- Publication of the IT plan, investment portfolio

Execution (administration):
- Implementation of IT projects
- IT Performance Management
- Human resources development, continuous improvement

Value (measurement):
- Measuring the impact of investments

The key questions that must be asked in each phase to ensure alignment between the IT plan and the company plan are:

- **Strategy:** Are we doing the right things?
    - Are the investments consistent with the business plan?
    - Are they compatible with the business principles?
    - Do they contribute to sustainable competitive advantages?
    - Do they provide value with an acceptable level of risk?

- **Execution:** Are we doing them right?
    - Are the solutions scalable?
    - Is the process of using and delivering services well defined?
    - Do we have enough qualified human resources?

- **Value:** Are we getting the benefits?
    - Is there a precise level of commitment from all parties?
    - Is it clear who is responsible for reaping the benefits of technologies?
    - Are there relevant and quantifiable metrics?

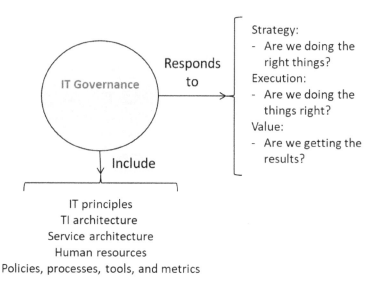

Figure 4.3.- Scope and reach of IT governance

The products and activities of each phase are:

- Strategy (meaning):
    - Aligning the IT plan with the business plan
    - Publication of the IT plan, investment portfolio

- Execution (administration):
    - Implementation of IT projects
    - IT Performance Management
    - Human resources development, continuous improvement

- Value (measurement):
    - Measuring the impact of investments

The role of the board of directors and senior management is: to ensure that the IT strategy is in line with the business strategy, assess whether IT is meeting its commitments, direct the IT strategy by controlling investments and supporting its projects, and finally ensure that there is a culture of collaboration between IT and the rest of the organization.

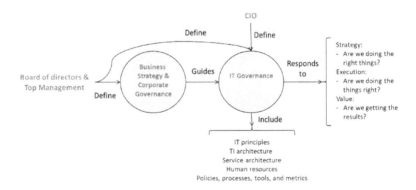

Figure 4.4.- A framework for IT governance

4.6.- Summary

- When people invest their money in a company, they expect that the organization's resources will be used in the best way to maximize the investor's profits and protect their assets.
- Corporate governance focuses on the combination of processes and structures implemented by the board of directors to inform, direct, manage and monitor the organization's activities to achieve its objectives.
- IT governance defines organizational structures and processes that ensure that IT supports and extends the organization's strategic objectives, promoting the best use of technologies for the company's purposes.
- The scope of IT governance includes IT principles, technological architecture, application architecture, service architecture, investment and prioritization plan, human resource development plan, policies, processes, tools, and techniques.

4.7.- Review exercises

Questions

1. What is corporate governance?
2. What is the difference between corporate governance and IT governance?
3. Why is it essential for a company to have IT governance?
4. What are the roles involved in defining and operating IT governance?
5. What are the components of IT governance?
6. What are the critical questions for each phase of IT governance?

Exercises

1. Identify three phrases that can be used in a company to define its technology strategy.
2. List three phrases that would demonstrate that the execution of the IT plan is working correctly.
3. Research some metrics used in the industry to measure the success of a technology application.

Chapter 5

Systems planning

"Not everything that counts can be counted, and not everything that can be counted counts."

William Bruce Cameron, "Informal Sociology" 1963

5.1.- Learning objectives

- Understand how to prioritize current projects and new developments.
- Identify and classify the necessary projects.
- Learn how to define infrastructure projects.
- Understand how to qualify projects with quantifiable costs and benefits.
- Understand how to qualify projects with non-quantifiable costs and benefits.
- Learn how to integrate a consolidated list of projects.

5.2.- Elements of an IT plan

The job of an organization's IT area is to help the company achieve its goals. A company's operation generally requires several different information systems. Payroll has to be paid, accounting cannot stop, and production must run uninterrupted. The main priority for the IT area is to keep the current systems functioning.

In addition to keeping the company running, the IT area must develop new projects to support future operations or improve current ones. New projects can be classified into three groups: mandatory projects, such as those that have to be done to meet some legal requirement; infrastructure projects, which are projects that leave no value in themselves but are required so that other projects work (examples of these would be communication networks or information security systems); and computer projects that support some strategic initiative of the organization.

Once the projects in which the IT area is going to work have been defined, the next step is to determine the hardware and software required, the necessary data management platforms, and the personnel and budget needed for the operation of the area.

5.3.- Current operation and new developments

As mentioned above, a company has information systems operating and a list of potential future information systems projects in the portfolio. The first responsibility of the IT area is to keep current projects running, followed by new developments to support the organization's plans.

To define which current projects require more attention, they can be categorized in a 2x2 table with two axes: the importance of the project for the company and the project's health (in terms of its operational stability). Those projects that are highly important and have poor health require immediate attention. It is essential that they are updated and do not stop operating. Healthy major projects should only be kept running. Unimportant systems in good health are at the bottom of the care list and can continue to run as long as they do not present a problem. Less critical systems with problems follow in the list. It is crucial to assess whether they should be maintained or eliminated.

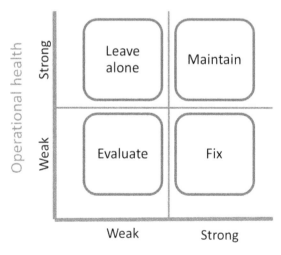

Figure 5.1.- Classification of current projects by importance and stability

5.4.- Necessary projects

Some technology projects can be justified in terms of their costs and benefits. However, some systems must be completed even if their price exceeds the expected tangible benefits. Three kinds of unprofitable projects must be considered in a company's IT plan: those that are required to comply with a legal requirement, infrastructure projects necessary to provide communications or data to other projects, and strategic projects that are necessary to maintain the level of competitiveness of the company or its public image.

The projects necessary to comply with any law or regulation must be included in the IT plan, and their delivery and implementation must be planned within the required times. Examples are systems that protect customer information, report certain activities to government offices, or notify the organization's results to shareholders.

Some necessary projects are those required for compliance with the Sarbanes Oxley Act (SOX), which is mandatory for any company listed on the New York Stock Exchange or operating in the United States. The law seeks to protect investors by improving the quality and accuracy of the financial information issued by the company and demands fines or even jail for non-compliance. Developing the systems to comply with this law is a top priority in any technology plan. Companies like Cemex (NYSE: CX) apply these principles and describe them on their websites [Cemex, 2021].

Mini-case: How to classify an information security project?

As part of the current information security program, the IT department requires antivirus software on all computers in the company. The procedures also force users to change their passwords from time to time. The measures appear to work; although two competitors fell victim to ransomware attacks, our company has never been attacked. However, the technology area insists that a considerable amount be invested in redundant data systems and copies of our files. Doing that can take resources away from other projects and does not add value to current operations. Should the company analyze this project seriously?

5.5.- Infrastructure projects

Sometimes, it is necessary to carry out specific projects to prepare the way, obtain data, or transport information needed for other projects. These are known as infrastructure projects. An analogy would be like building a road to get to a city. The road itself does not produce any revenue, but having it will allow the operation of businesses in different areas.

When an infrastructure project is necessary for a single strategic project, the infrastructure project should be considered part of the cost of the project it serves, and this must be completed just before the project requires it.

On the other hand, if the infrastructure project enables several new initiatives, it should be considered a strategic project in itself and compete for resources with the other strategic projects of the company.

Either way, an infrastructure project can wait until just before the first project it serves plans to start operating.

Mini-case: A Tale of Two Cities

There are two projects on the to-do list of a business intelligence specialist on a sports team. The first is a system to analyze why 20% of fans with full-season tickets in the box area decide not to attend the games. The second is a system to analyze why 10% of the fans in the preferred seats of the stadium chose not to renew their annual subscription this year. How can both projects be prioritized? Which one needs attention first? Why?

5.6.- Quantifiable strategic projects

A new system requires an investment in software and building the interfaces between the new system and the systems already in operation. Additionally, the company might have to purchase new computer equipment if the one in use is not powerful enough to operate the new system. Another cost is the training of the staff who would be working with the new system.

The decision to approve or not a project depends on many factors. It's not just based on the cost of the software. Although the project was so expensive that it was not within reach of the company, the only alternative would be to reject the project and look for a solution more in line with the possibilities of the business.

Assuming the company had the money to pay for the project, the next question is: what benefits does it bring? And how complicated is it for the project to work? A project that is too expensive and does not produce benefits is easy to refuse. Similarly, projects that wouldn't work are also quickly rejected.

Analyzing whether a project is suitable for an organization requires calculating its costs (both tangible and intangible) and its benefits (tangible and intangible), in addition to the risk involved in its implementation. The analysis should be done for a period equivalent to the project's expected useful life (so if the project is expected to operate for five years, the costs and benefits must be calculated for that entire period). With this information, it is easier to decide whether or not the new system should be approved.

Once the costs and benefits of a project have been identified, the marginal costs and benefits are calculated, that is, the additional costs and benefits that would occur if the project were not implemented.

If a system helps sell $1,200,000 worth of products, but the company already sells $1,000,000, then the new system only provides a marginal benefit of $200,000 in upselling. If the company decides not to implement the project, it already has sales of one million dollars. The marginal benefit is the additional benefit to what you already have. In this case, when calculating the sales profits of the project, it only contributes $200,000, not $1,200,000.

If a company already has a computer and the new system runs on the same equipment (there is no need to expand or buy additional parts), the cost of equipment for the project is zero. Similarly, if the company already pays rent for some office space, and the new system operates in the same facilities, the marginal cost for office space is zero.

On the other hand, if the software can run on the current equipment but requires a memory expansion of $ 100,000, the cost of equipment for the project is not the cost of the computer that is already had, but only the additional hundred thousand that would have to be disbursed to operate the software.

Marginal costs are those additional costs to those that already have that are required to carry out a project. A project is analyzed solely in terms of its marginal costs and benefits.

A relatively easy way to understand the costs and benefits of a project is by using a timetable to indicate the cash flows (money inflows and outflows). The lifespan of a project can be divided into years, quarters, or months (depending on the expected scope). Costs and benefits are listed in the first column; each additional column represents a timeslot (month, quarter, or year, according to the detail of analysis desired).

There may be lines with subtotals of costs incurred and benefits received. The last line lists the cash flow of each period obtained by subtracting the charges from the benefits.

Table 5.1.- Cash flow of a project

	1	2	3	4	5	6	7	8	9	10	TOTAL
Marginal costs											
remodeling	30000	10000									
equipment	10000	30000									
legal costs	10000										
operation	5000	5000	2000	2000	2000	2000	2000	2000	2000	2000	
Total costs	55000	45000	2000	2000	2000	2000	2000	2000	2000	2000	116000
Marginal benefits											
sales	0	8000	11000	11000	11000	11000	11000	11000	11000	11000	
travel expenses	0	0	1500	3000	3000	3000	3000	3000	3000	3000	
Total benefits	0	8000	12500	14000	14000	14000	14000	14000	14000	14000	118500
Net flow	-55000	-37000	10500	12000	12000	12000	12000	12000	12000	12000	2500

Once the costs and benefits of implementing a new information system are identified, it is possible to calculate the proposal's net present value and internal rate of return [Baca Urbina, 2015, Alanís, 2021]. In the alternative presented, as initially proposed, year 1 requires an investment of $ 55,000, year two needs $45,000, and the expense for years 3 to 10 is $2,000. The project produces no benefits in year one, $8,000 in year two, and $12,000 for years three to ten.

The calculation requires including a line with the net flow of each period. The net flow is calculated by adding the income and subtracting the expenses of each period. So the flow of year 1 is negative (-$55,000), and that of year 6 (for example) is positive ($12,000).

Assuming that the +Minimum Acceptable Rate of Return (MARR, or hurdle Rate) for the company is 10%, the formula for calculating the NPV is **=B16+NPV(B18,C16:K16)**, and for calculating the IRR is **=IRR(B16:K16,0)**

In this case, the results show that the project has an NPV of -$31,676.84 and an IRR of 0.5229%. This result is much lower than the expected MARR (which, in this case, could be 10%), so this project, as presented, would be rejected.

	A	B	C	D	E	F	G	H	I	J	K	L	M	N
4		1	2	3	4	5	6	7	8	9	10		TOTAL	
5	Marginal costs													
6	remodeling	30000	10000											
7	equipment	10000	30000											
8	legal costs	10000												
9	operation	5000	5000	2000	2000	2000	2000	2000	2000	2000	2000			
10	Total costs	55000	45000	2000	2000	2000	2000	2000	2000	2000	2000		116000	
11	Marginal benefits													
12	sales	0	8000	11000	11000	11000	11000	11000	11000	11000	11000			
13	travel expenses	0	0	1500	3000	3000	3000	3000	3000	3000	3000			
14	Total benefits	0	8000	12500	14000	14000	14000	14000	14000	14000	14000		118500	
15														
16	Net flow	-55000	-37000	10500	12000	12000	12000	12000	12000	12000	12000		2500	
17														
18														
19	MARR	10.000%		Minimum Acceptable Rate of Return										
20	NPV	-$31,677		Net Present Value (difference between the project's value and the minimum acceptable return)										
21	IRR	0.5229%		Internal Rate of Return (interest paid by the project)										
22														

Figure 5.2.- Financial analysis of an investment project

If a new estimate considers that sales for years three to ten three can go up to $22,000 while keeping all other parameters intact, then the new NPV is $21,672.42 (positive), and the IRR is 15.4247% (better than the MARR of 10). This version of the project would be acceptable.

	A	B	C	D	E	F	G	H	I	J	K	L	M	N
4		1	2	3	4	5	6	7	8	9	10		TOTAL	
5	Marginal costs													
6	remodeling	30000	10000											
7	equipment	10000	30000											
8	legal costs	10000												
9	operation	5000	5000	2000	2000	2000	2000	2000	2000	2000	2000			
10	Total costs	55000	45000	2000	2000	2000	2000	2000	2000	2000	2000		116000	
11	Marginal benefits													
12	sales	0	8000	22000	22000	22000	22000	22000	22000	22000	22000			
13	travel expenses	0	0	1500	3000	3000	3000	3000	3000	3000	3000			
14	Total benefits	0	8000	23500	25000	25000	25000	25000	25000	25000	25000		206500	
15														
16	Net flow	-55000	-37000	21500	23000	23000	23000	23000	23000	23000	23000		90500	
17														
18														
19	MARR	10.000%		Minimum Acceptable Rate of Return										
20	NPV	$21,672		Net Present Value (difference between the project's value and the minimum acceptable return)										
21	IRR	15.4247%		Internal Rate of Return (interest paid by the project)										
22														

Figure 5.3.- Variation in the financial analysis of a project

A common practice is to present three scenarios in each proposal: the expected scenario, the optimistic scenario, and a pessimistic scenario (most likely, best case, and worst case). Assuming for this project a pessimistic scenario where sales in year three rise to only $18,000; the most likely alternative presenting sales of $20,000 and the best case with sales of $22,000 keeping everything else constant, the results would be as follows:

Table 5.2.- IRR of three possible expected sales scenarios

Scenario	Expected sales starting year 3	NPV (MARR=10%)	IRR
Worst case	$18,000	$2,272.69	10.6002%
Expected	$20,000	$11,972.56	13.0745%
Best case	$22,000	$21,672.42	15.4247%

Since, in this case, all the scenarios are favorable, the project would be approved under these conditions.

Sometimes, the pessimistic scenario can result in a loss, while the expected and optimistic ones give positive results. In this case, it is essential to assess the level of risk and the probability of each scenario. The risk analysis should help determine whether or not to proceed with the project.

How valid are the results?

Excel is a powerful tool, and if a project is not presenting the necessary results for approval, it is very tempting to change the profit estimate so that the final result is acceptable. This practice is dangerous because obtaining the results promised in the modified analysis might prove challenging.

It is convenient to determine the effort necessary for a project to be profitable when an analysis is modified. For example, if a project needs sales in year three of at least $18,000 for the MPV and IRR to be favorable, we must ask ourselves how difficult it would be to reach $18,000 in sales. If the answer, in all honesty, is that this number is no problem, then you can present the project to the authorities that analyze it and request the budget to carry it out. If, on the other hand, we find that reaching $18,000 in sales requires an extraordinary effort that has never been achieved before, the project will likely never deliver the results needed to be considered profitable.

It is much better to identify a potential problem when the project is in the planning and analysis stage than to wait for implementation to realize that the wrong decision has been made.

A good analysis can provide confidence that the project has potential and allow decision-makers to compare different investment alternatives. IRR and NPV will enable you to compare the expected results of diverse projects such as technology, marketing, or production, to name a few. These analyses will allow us to make the best decision for the organization's future.

5.7.- Non-quantifiable strategic projects

If a project does not produce tangible benefits, the methodology for classifying it is to grade it using a points system according to predefined criteria. [Alanís, 2020]

As an example, in this chapter, the criteria for prioritizing projects are based on four main factors:

- the importance of the program that the project supports,
- how important is the technology's support for the project,
- the availability of the technology and
- what disposition users have.

However, each company is different and can define another group of factors to qualify.

In this case, the First Factor rates the project in general:

The importance of the program: It is evident that if, for example, the project to identify new customers is more critical in the organization's plan than the project to eliminate queues in the information desk in a store, then the computer programs for the first would take precedence over those of the second. There is usually a list of priority programs in the company, and there is an order between them. This list can be assigned points. The points given to an overall initiative can be a first indicator of where attention should be when planning new projects.

Table 5.3.- General list of projects with scoring

Project	Importance	Points
A	1	85
B	2	83
C	3	75
D	4	68
E	5	56

The following three factors qualify the computer science role within that project:

The level of computer support: There are projects where having a computer is indispensable for its operation. Let's mention, for example, the project to modernize the management of customer credits; this could not be done without the support of computer systems. On the other hand, some projects may not depend so much on technology, for example, the project to improve employees' health by organizing a baseball league. In these cases, although the sports league project may be more critical in some list of projects, probably the modernization of credit management project should receive greater attention from the IT area since that is where the most significant benefit would be obtained from the investment.

The availability of technology: An essential factor in defining whether a project is done this year or the following year is whether the technology it requires is available in the organization or even in the market. If I already have the computer, it may be easier to get the software. On the other hand, technologies are generally more accessible as time goes on. Working with a technology that is just being developed can be expensive and not give the expected results. However, projects rejected last year as too costly or too difficult may be viable this year, given the market changes and new developments.

The fourth factor to consider is *the users' disposition*: Under similar circumstances, it is easier to implement a project for a user who wants it to succeed than for a user who is reluctant to change.

By placing the three factors in a table, you can qualify each project in terms of each element. So, if a project requires full computer support receives 10 points in that factor. A project that needs technology that is unavailable or difficult to find could get 3 points in the corresponding line.

Table 5.4.- Projects qualified by value

Project	Importance of technology	Availability of technology	User's disposition
A	8	10	8
B	10	10	9
C	9	8	8
D	4	3	9
E	8	10	5

The first step in analyzing non-quantifiable projects is assigning a weight to each identified factor. The sum of all elements should be 100. The next step is to calculate, for each project, the percentage value of IT in the program by multiplying the grade obtained by the project on each category times its respective weight. The resulting number is the percentage contribution, which is then multiplied by the program's points on the general plan. A project with a grade of 10 on each item should get 100% of the program's value. A project with 50% on each item should get half of the points available for the program.

Table 5.5.- Projects with the calculation of the value of the contribution of technology in each one

Project	Importance of technology	Availability of technology	User's disposition	IT Value
Weight →	50%	30%	20%	
A	8	10	8	0.86
B	10	10	9	0.98
C	9	8	8	0.85
D	4	3	9	0.47
E	8	10	5	0.80

Combining the percentage of IT contribution for each project (From table 5.5) with the overall project's points (from table 5.3) yields a score indicating each project's importance within the year's IT plan.

Table 5.5.- Projects with a score indicating the importance of the technology area

Project	Importance of technology	Availability of technology	User's disposition	IT Value	Project's initial points	IT points
Weight →	50%	30%	20%			
A	8	10	8	0.86	85	73.1
B	10	10	9	0.98	83	81.3
C	9	8	8	0.85	75	63.8
D	4	3	9	0.47	68	32.0
E	8	10	5	0.80	56	44.8

This calculation allows you to reorder projects differently from the global list. For example, in this case, although project A has higher priority than project B, the latter has more points for the IT department, so it deserves more attention.

Table 5.6.- Projects are ordered according to their importance in the technology area

Project	IT points
B	81.3
A	73.1
C	63.8
E	44.8
D	32.0

The resulting list of ordered projects is not final. You have to consider the resources and budget available and decide which project could be completed, starting from the project with the highest score.

5.8.- Integration of the project plan

The final project plan consists of the sum of the projects to keep the current platform running and the new projects, consisting of strategic and infrastructure projects, both quantifiable and non-quantifiable.

The list of projects created with this methodology becomes a tool for negotiation. Considering factors such as the balance of risks (we can not take only long-term or easy projects), you can start negotiating with the users to define a final IS development plan.

5.9.- Summary

- The first responsibility of the IT area is to keep current projects running, followed by new developments to support the organization's plans.
- To define which current projects require more attention, they can be categorized in a 2x2 table with two axes: the importance of the project for the company and the project's health (in terms of its operational stability).
- New projects can be classified in terms of their costs and benefits.
- There are three kinds of unprofitable projects that must be considered in the work plan: those that are required to comply with a legal requirement; infrastructure projects necessary to provide communications or data to other projects; and strategic projects that are necessary to maintain the level of competitiveness of the company or its public image.
- Analyzing a quantifiable project requires identifying its marginal costs and benefits and using them to calculate its net present value (NPV) and internal rate of return (IRR).
- As an analysis of a project requires estimates of future flows, a common practice is to present three scenarios in each proposal: the most likely, best case and worst case.
- A good analysis can provide confidence that the project has potential and allow decision-makers to compare different investment alternatives.
- If the benefits of a project cannot be quantified, the methodology for classifying it is to assign points according to predefined criteria.
- The final project plan consists of the sum of the projects to keep the current platform running and the new projects, consisting of

strategic and infrastructure projects, both quantifiable and non-quantifiable.

- The list of projects created with this methodology becomes a tool for negotiation. Considering factors such as the balance of risks (we can not take only long-term or easy projects), you can start negotiating with the users to define a final IS development plan.

5.10.- Review exercises

Questions

1. Why is it important to focus first on keeping current projects working before thinking about new developments?
2. What should be done with critical but unstable current projects?
3. What should be done with operating projects that are not very important and relatively stable?
4. What priority should government-required projects (like a new tax) have?
5. How to decide when to plan an infrastructure project?
6. What can be concluded from the internal rate of return of a project?
7. Why is it important to analyze a project's most likely, best-case, and worst-case scenarios?
8. How can you use IRR and VPN to evaluate a computer project?
9. What criteria can be used to evaluate projects with non-quantifiable benefits?

Exercises

1. Identify two technology infrastructure projects in a company.
2. Identify three mandatory projects in an organization.
3. A computer project requires an investment of 50,000 in the first year and 30,000 in the second year, producing profits of 10,000 in the third year and 15,000 during years four to ten (which is when its useful life ends). What is the internal rate of return for that project?
4. List two projects with quantifiable and two with non-quantifiable benefits that are in operation in a company.

Chapter 6

Measurement of Results

"I believe evidence. I believe in observation, measurement, and reasoning, confirmed by independent observers. I'll believe anything, no matter how wild and ridiculous, if there is evidence for it. The wilder and more ridiculous something is, however, the firmer and more solid the evidence will have to be."

Isaac Asimov, "The Roving Mind" 1983.

6.1.- Learning objectives

- Explain why it is hard to measure IT results.
- Recognize the effect of time on the value of technology.
- Recognize the effect of risks on the impacts of technology.
- Identify indicators of investment in technology.
- Identify indicators of technological assets.
- Understand how to measure the result of IT use, organizational performance, and risk on IT indicators.

6.2.- The importance of measuring results

The primary responsibility of the IT area in an organization is to operate existing systems and develop new IT solutions to support corporate strategies. For that reason, as soon as the IT area finishes one project, it starts the next without looking back or stopping to analyze the results obtained. The problem with this position is that it limits organizational learning (we don't know if things are being done well or how to improve) and complicates getting funding for future projects (there is no evidence that investments are producing the expected results).

The main excuse for not measuring the results of technology is that there is no time. The real reason is that results are difficult to quantify. While it is easy to define a measure for the number of computers or the range of the network, the value that a system brings to the company is not so simple to determine. For example, a CRM system helps the sales area to be more effective. However, who gets the credit if there is an increase in sales? Are the benefits attributable to increase effort or to better information?

An added pressure to reporting results comes from the demand for increased measurements by senior management. In most organizations, senior management faces pressures to reduce operating costs and justify all investments, so technological projects must compete for resources just as all other company projects [Kohli, Sherer, and Barton, 2003].

6.3.- The different dimensions of the impact of technology on organizations

Some information systems have quantifiable impacts, such as a process optimization system, where it is easy to measure savings for the organization. On the other hand, some systems provide value in support for other areas, which, combined with other internal and external factors, help improve results. In these cases, the improvements cannot be directly attributed to the technology (although it can be argued that without technology, there would be no results).

Additionally, the benefit of a system may not appear until sometime after it has started operations. Users need training, customers need to get used to innovations, and historical data needs to be updated so that the new system operates as expected. For example, in the pharmaceutical industry, an investment to create an information reporting and analysis system require investment in technology to create the application. The system produces the reports, which allows for analysis, which then impacts patient management and eventually results in profits for the company. Figure 6.1 shows a diagram of this case.

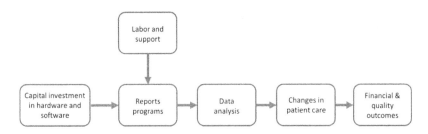

Figure 6.1.- Impact of a computer investment over time in a pharmaceutical company. Source: Devaraj and Kohli [2000]

An analysis of the pharmaceutical industry's case and other similar cases shows four aspects to consider for measuring the impacts of technology on organizations: investment in technology, technological assets, the direct effect of technology, and the impact on organizational performance. Figure 6.2 shows the relationship between these elements.

Figure 6.2.- Aspects to consider to measure the impacts of technology in the organizations. Source: Kohli and Sherer [2002]

Risk is another critical factor deriving from the use of technology in organizations. Information technology can make a company more reliable. On the other hand, it can also make it vulnerable to cyber-attacks or technological failures. Each element of technology included in a project can vary the risk balance of the company. It is essential to quantify the level of risk to validate the impact of the technology on the organization and define strategies to manage or contain it. Figure 6.3 shows the different risk elements around each effect to be analyzed.

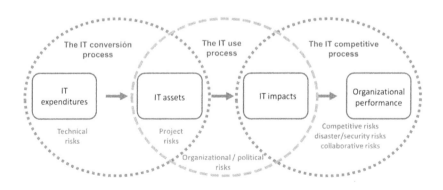

Figure 6.3.- Risks of technology impacts on organizations. Source: Kohli and Sherer [2002]

6.4.- IT expenditures

One of the most quantifiable elements is the investment in technology and the budget of the information systems area. This indicator includes hardware, software, communications, training, and personnel. It is advisable to separate the amounts dedicated to current systems operation and new developments. It could also be valuable to separate investments by functional area of the company.

A table with the budget data is a moment in time that can be interesting, but it is more valuable to see how those values have varied over various periods. It may also be interesting to compare our company's investments in technology with those of other companies in the same field. Compared to the same indicator in similar organizations, the percentage of technology spending on the company's total revenue can indicate whether there is an over- or under-investment problem. Technology spending information is different in each type of industry. While some markets rely on technology, others might consider IT as just another tool.

In Mexico, it is reported that companies, on average, allocate just under 2% of their total revenue to invest in technology [NetSD, 2019]. The number is considered low, but it provides a benchmark for analysis.

Among the indicators to be analyzed are:

- Total IT Budget
- Staff salaries
- Operating expenses
- Spending on training
- Maintenance costs
- Investment in hardware
- Investment in telecommunications
- Investment in system software
- Investment in applications

It is acceptable to assume that a company that invests in technology finds value in the solutions provided, but other factors also influence the results.

6.5.- IT assets

Generally, the first activity in the systems planning process is carrying out an inventory of operating computer equipment, networks, and software. The survey shows the current state of the company in terms of technology. It is essential to keep this information up to date to see the evolution of technology adoption in the company and compare it against market standards.

The company's technological assets include hardware, software, embedded systems, and communications. From a hardware standpoint, it's important to catalog the number of servers, workstations, and peripherals available and see their evolution over time. One metric that compares companies is the number of workstations or PCs per employee. In some businesses, the number should be 1-1 or better; in others, it could be up to one computer for every ten employees, depending on the type of industry.

Software analysis should catalog applications into standard applications and custom-made applications. Projects under development are listed on a timeline to see the expected delivery dates of each of their modules.

Another important indicator is the age of each piece of hardware and software. Old technology platforms can become time bombs ready to fail at the worst possible time. The same goes for software. Legacy software has been modified countless times, can already be incomprehensible, and suffers a catastrophic failure following minor maintenance adjustments. Sometimes it's convenient to rewrite an old piece of software to simplify subsequent maintenance.

6.6.- IT impacts

This series of indicators refer more to the direct impacts of technology on the company. The number of customers served, transactions processed, website visits, completed orders, total sales cycle time, and the number of exceptions requested are measured.

From a process point of view, you can measure the projects you have worked on, the hours invested, the departments involved, change initiatives, and training courses offered.

Regarding data analysis and decision support, indicators such as the number of queries, special reports requested, and workstations in use by executives can be significant.

For the IT area, an important indicator of its performance is the opinion of its users. Satisfied users are an indicator of good performance and good results. If this indicator is considered relevant, it is vital to implement project exit surveys and periodic customer feedback reviews on operating applications.

6.7.- Organizational performance

Organizational performance indicators can be harder to identify because technology's benefits are not often straightforward. In many cases, the benefits come from using the information produced by the system and include elements beyond the technology area's control. However, it is vital to analyze the quantity, quality, and timeliness of the information being provided and the number and distribution of users in the organization.

Some measurements include the elements of competitiveness that were set as objectives during the systems planning phase, the company's market share, customer opinion, awards received, and even the price of the company's stock. These indicators can provide interesting data on the impact of technology on the organization.

Mini-case: Who gets the medal?

In 2019, at the initiative of the systems area, the sales manager attended a technology conference and found an application that could improve customer telephone service. Upon receiving a call, based on the number from the caller ID system, the customer could be identified. If the customer is already registered, the sales agent could see all their history on the screen before the customer says their first word.

After great effort in the systems and sales areas, the software started operation at the beginning of 2020. In March 2020, the world faced a health emergency due to the COVID-19 virus, and people had to isolate themselves. Phone sales skyrocketed.

Did the health emergency cause an increase in sales? Was it because the company was ready with technology to increase online sales? Or was the sales staff responsible for being at the right place at the right time? Who deserves the credit?

In Mexico, a place with great mountain scenes is the Paso de Cortes. Named in honor of Hernan Cortes, it is a strategic point that connects central Mexico with the Golf coast. It is 3600 meters above sea level and surrounded by majestic mountains: the Popocatepetl and the Iztaccihuatl.

Several banks used that route to lay their data lines since this was a strategic communication point for Mexico. However, both mountains surrounding Paso de Cortez are volcanoes. After being asleep for much of the twentieth century, Popocatepetl became active in 1991, and the Mexican Government had to prepare evacuation plans in case of a major eruption.

The banks realized their operation depended on a communication line that crossed a possible lava flow and had to analyze their risk tolerance.

Should these banks rethink their investment strategy in communications?

6.8.- Risks

As discussed above, there are different types of risks in operating a company [Kohli and Sherer, 2002]

- **Technical risks:** Failures in technology may occur, and the company may be offline for some time.
- **Project risks:** Many IT projects are delayed by failures in specifications or the complexity of the proposed solutions.
- **Organizational and political risks:** Failures in implementing organizational changes can cause a system to be misused. Sometimes, shifts in the balance of political forces in the organization can also affect how people use the system.
- **Competitive risks:** Some competitors may gain access to confidential information or change competitive market forces.
- **Security risks/disasters:** There may be vulnerability to cyber-attacks or failures caused by natural disasters such as fires, floods, or earthquakes in the locality of the data centers.
- **Collaboration risks:** Information needed to collaborate may not be available or shared correctly.

Technology can work to increase or reduce some of these risks. It is essential to measure the organization's exposure to possible threats based on the applications and the technological configurations in use.

6.9.- Which is the most important indicator?

All the indicators say something about the operation of technology in the organization. However, unless yours is a large company with full-time staff dedicated to collecting indicators, you will likely have to choose those most relevant indicators to track and report as results of the IT area to senior management.

Three areas are generally of interest to shareholders: Impact on revenue, efficiency improvements, and risk reduction [Naegle and Ganly, 2020]. The suggestion is to choose three to five indicators from each category as a starting point to show the impact of the technology.

Other indicators, such as budget and assets, might not be critical for shareholders initially but should also be collected to measure the overall health of systems in the company.

One recommendation is that it is preferable to measure something than not to measure anything. Start by reporting something, even a simple measure, and as you see value in the information, and receive feedback from senior management, improve your indicators. The quality of your reports can improve over time, and those indicators that provide a better idea of the performance of the IT area can be gradually included.

6.10.- Summary

- Measuring the results and impact of technology on the organization is essential to show if things are being done well and to show evidence that investments in IT are producing the expected results.
- It is difficult to measure results because they can be intermingled with organizational performance, it can take time before seeing the results, and they can change the balance of risks in the organization.

- Among the indicators to consider are:
    - IT expenditure
    - IT assets (number and age)
    - IT Impacts
    - Organizational performance
    - Risks
- It is preferable to measure something than not to measure anything.
- Start by reporting something, even a simple measure, and as you see value in the information, and receive feedback from senior management, improve your indicators.
- The quality of your reports can improve over time, and those indicators that provide a better idea of the performance of the IT area can be gradually included.

6.11.- Review exercises

Questions

1. Why is performance measurement important?
2. Why is it challenging to measure IT results?
3. What are the most relevant indicators of the following elements?:
    - Investment in technology
    - Technological assets (number and age)
    - IT Impact
    - Organizational performance
    - Risks

Exercises

1. Look for indicators of technology investment as a percentage of sales in different industries.
2. Look for indicators of technology penetration in companies (usage and volume).
3. Interview a TI professional and ask them what indicators the IT area in their company reports.

Part III

IT Delivery and Support

Chapter 7

COBIT

"Why, you might ask, didn't I recognize the above facts before September 11? The answer, sadly, is that I did - but I didn't convert thought into action. I violated the Noah rule: Predicting rain doesn't count; building arks does."

Warren Buffett, Director's Letter to Shareholders, Berkshire Hathaway, Inc., February 2002.

7.1.- Learning objectives

- Recognize the elements of COBIT and its importance.
- Understand how the COBIT standard has evolved.
- Recognize COBIT's objectives in IT corporate governance and IT management.
- Identify COBIT domains and targets.
- Understand, in general terms, the components of the description of each COBIT objective.

7.2.- What is COBIT?

COBIT (Control Objectives for Information and Related Technology) is a framework for IT governance and management designed to help organizations create value from their IT initiatives, better manage their risks, and optimize their resources [ISACA, 2018-2].

Initially published in 1996, COBIT was a framework for technology auditing. However, the idea was that the model would evolve in stages. In 1998, COBIT 2 provided additional guidance on IT controls. COBIT 3 was launched as a management framework in 2000. COBIT 4 in 2005 was a complete IT governance framework. COBIT 5 was established in 2012 as a comprehensive framework of globally accepted practices, analytical tools, and models and included enhancements to align overall business strategy with IT strategy. Most recently, ISACA introduced COBIT 2019 in late 2018, using a maturity model based on the integration of CMMI's capacity maturity model and including updates aligned with the latest industry standards, as well as a design guide that helps organizations adapt a governance system to their needs [ISACA, 2023-2].

Among the advantages offered by COBIT is that it is a unique framework that reaches from governance to administration. It is a model that has matured over time and has a business perspective that allows it to expand its impact beyond IT.

What COBIT does not do, is fully describe the entire area of information technology of the company, nor is it a frame of reference to manage all the technology of the organization. Additionally, COBIT is not a frame of reference for organizing business processes [Lainhart, 2018].

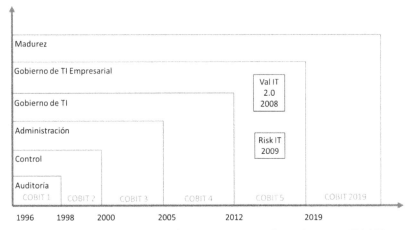

Figure 7.1.- Evolution of COBIT. Adapted from Harmer [2013].

7.3.- Domains and objectives of COBIT

A feature of the latest version of COBIT is that it separates IT corporate governance from IT management [ISACA, 2018-1].

IT corporate governance ensures that:

- Shareholder needs, conditions, and options are assessed to determine balanced and agreed-on business objectives.
- Prioritization and decision-making set the direction to follow.
- Performance and compliance are measured against the agreed direction and objectives.

IT management plans, builds, executes, and supervises activities in line with the direction set by the governing body to achieve the company's objectives.

COBIT identifies 40 objectives that can be grouped into five domains, four of them in administration and one in governance:

- Governance objectives
  - EDM – Evaluate, Direct, and Monitor
- Management Objectives
  - APO – Align, Plan and Organize
  - BAI – Build, Acquire, Implement
  - DSS – Deliver, Service and Support
  - MEA - Monitor, Evaluate and Assess

One focus of some consulting firms is to help organizations move from strategic planning to results of operation. In the world of COBIT, this represents the path from EDM to MEA [Edmead, 2020].

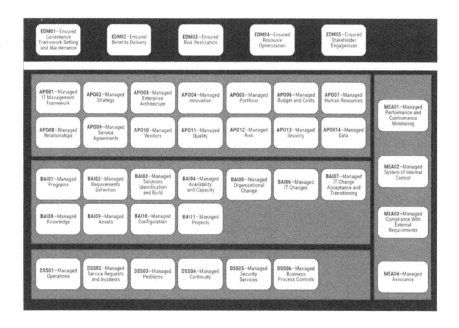

Figure 7.2.- COBIT Governance and Administration Objectives [ISACA, 2018-1]

7.4.- Detailed information on each objective

The document describes each of the 40 objectives.

For each objective, the following is specified:

-. High-level information

A. Processes
B. Organizational Structure
C. Information Flows
D. People, Skills, and Competencies
E. Policies and Procedures
F. Culture, Ethics, and Behavior
G. Services, Infrastructure, and Applications

High-level information

High-level information describes, in general terms, the objective, its focus, and its purpose. The information detailed in the reference framework for each of the objectives includes:

- Domain name
- Focus area
- Name of the objective (governance or administration)
- Description
- Purpose
- Business and alignment objectives
- Examples of metrics

One of the features of COBIT is that it provides detailed information on business and alignment objectives, as well as metrics that can be used for each. These goals form a cascade. Shareholder needs become business strategies that become alignment objectives that guide governance or management objectives.

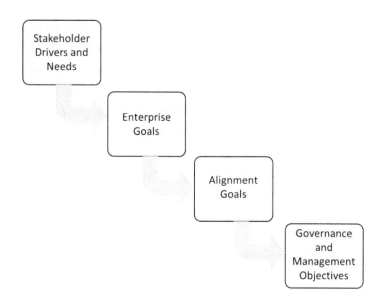

Figure 7.3.- Cascade of objectives [Edmead, 2020]

For example, the APO03 – Managed Enterprise Architecture objective carries the following data [ISACA, 2018-1]:

- Domain name: Align, Plan and Organize
- Focus Area: COBIT Core Model
- Target Name (governance or administration): APO03 — Managed Enterprise Architecture
- Description: Establish a common architecture consisting of business process, information, data, application and technology architecture layers. Create key models and practices that describe the baseline and target architectures, in line with the enterprise and I&T strategy. Define requirements for taxonomy, standards, guidelines, procedures, templates and tools, and provide a linkage for these components. Improve alignment, increase agility, improve quality of information and generate potential cost savings through initiatives such as re-use of building block components.
- Purpose: Represent the different building blocks that make up the enterprise and its interrelationships as well as the principles guiding their design and evolution over time, to enable a standard, responsive and efficient delivery of operational and strategic objectives.

The document then shows the business and alignment objectives, followed by example metrics for each. In this case, the business objectives of APO03 - Managed Enterprise Architecture are:

- EG01 Portfolio of competitive products and services
- EG05 Customer-oriented service culture
- EG08 Optimizing the functionality of internal business processes
- EG12 Managed Digital Transformation Programs

And the alignment goals are:

- AG06 Agility to turn business requirements into operational solutions
- AG08 Enable and support business processes by integrating applications and technology

A. Processes

The following section in each objective is to describe the processes that compose it. For each process, the following are listed:

- Management practice
- Example metrics
- Activities
- Related guidance (standards, frameworks, compliance, requirements)
- Detailed reference

For the APO03 – Managed Enterprise Architecture objective, five processes are included:

- APO03.01 Develop the enterprise architecture vision.
- APO03.02 Define reference architecture.
- APO03.03 Select opportunities and solutions.
- APO03.04 Define architecture implementation.
- APO03.05 Provide enterprise architecture services.

B. Organizational Structure

The organizational structure is presented in a matrix where the processes identified in the previous section are placed on the vertical axis. The organizational structures or individual roles are listed on the horizontal axis. The intersection of the two axes shows the level of responsibility of each unit/individual for each process. The types of responsibility are:

- **Responsible (R):** It is in charge of operating the practice and producing the results.

- **Accountable (A):** It is ultimately responsible for the work done. This type of responsibility cannot be delegated.

- **Consulted (C):** Provides information for practice.

- **Informed (I):** Receives information on the results.

Figure 7.4 shows the organizational structure table for the APO03 – Managed Enterprise Architecture objective.

B. Component: Organizational Structures	Chief Operating Officer	Chief Information Officer	Chief Technology Officer	Chief Digital Officer	I&T Governance Board	Architecture Board	Data Management Function	Head Architect
Key Management Practice								
APO03.01 Develop the enterprise architecture vision.		R	R	R	R	A	R	R
APO03.02 Define reference architecture.		R	R	R	R	A	R	R
APO03.03 Select opportunities and solutions.		R	R	R	R	A	R	R
APO03.04 Define architecture implementation.	R	R	R	R	R	A	R	R
APO03.05 Provide enterprise architecture services.	R	R	R	R	R	A		R

Related Guidance (Standards, Frameworks, Compliance Requirements)	Detailed Reference
The Open Group Standard TOGAF version 9.2, 2018	41. Architecture Board

Figure 7.4.- Table of organizational structure for the objective APO03 – Managed Enterprise Architecture [ISACA 2018].

C. Information Flows

The information flows section lists the elements of information linked to the practice. Each process has inputs and outputs. The table shows the description of the item and its source or destination.

Each process belonging to the objective "APO03 – Managed Enterprise Architecture" has information flows. For example, the process "APO03.01 Developing the enterprise architecture vision" has, among others, an input called Business Strategy, which comes from outside COBIT, and among its outputs are the architecture principles, whose destination is the processes BAI02.01, BAI03.01 and BAI03.02.

D. People, Skills, and Competences

This section identifies the human resources needed to execute the processes and the skills each participant must have. The example in this section lists five skills required by people involved in these processes: architecture design, data analysis, enterprise and business architecture, product / service planning, and solution architecture.

E. Policies and Procedures

This section lists policies and procedures that are relevant to the objective. The policy's name, description, related guide, and detailed reference are listed. In the case of "APO03.01 Developing the vision of enterprise architecture", "architecture principles" are listed as relevant policy, and reference is made to TOGAF version 9.2, 2018.

F. Culture, Ethics, and Behavior

This segment provides a guide to the cultural elements within the organization that support the achievement of the goal. In the example that is being discussed in this section, the item listed is:

> Create an environment in which management understands architectural needs relative to business goals and objectives. Drive effective practice of enterprise architecture throughout the organization (not only by enterprise architects). Ensure a holistic approach that links components more seamlessly (e.g., by moving away from dedicated teams of application specialists).

G. Services, Infrastructure, and Applications

This section lists third-party applications, equipment, or services that could support achieving the goals. For the case of "APO03.01 Developing the Vision of Enterprise Architecture", the listed application is an architecture repository.

7.5.- Success stories using COBIT

ISACA, the organization maintaining the COBIT standard, publishes case studies on its website describing how companies worldwide have successfully used the framework [ISACA, 2023-1]. Information is available at: https://www.isaca.org/resources/cobit/cobit-case-studies Among the most interesting cases are the following:

Mini-case: European Network of Electricity Transmission System Operators (ENTSO-E) [Volders and Jong, 2016].

The IT director of the European Network of Transmission System Operators for Electricity (ENTSO-E) undertook a pragmatic approach toward implementing COBIT 5 at the organization beginning in 2014.

Taking a practical approach towards implementing a program for the governance of enterprise IT (GEIT) based on COBIT 5, ENTSO-E focused on prioritizing the processes, the development of these processes, and—most important—the practical issues to overcome during the implementation of a new way of working. For more information, see: https://www.isaca.org/resources/news-and-trends/industry-news/2016/implementing-cobit-5-at-entso-e

---

7.6.- Summary

- COBIT (Control Objectives for Information and Related Technology) is a framework for IT governance and management designed to help organizations create value from their IT initiatives, manage risks, and optimize their resources.
- COBIT identifies 40 objectives that can be grouped into five domains, four of them in administration and one in governance:
  - Governance objectives
    - EDM – Evaluate, Direct, and Monitor
  - Management Objectives
    - APO – Align, Plan and Organize
    - BAI – Build, Acquire, Implement
    - DSS – Deliver, Serve and Support
    - MEA - Monitor, Evaluate and Measure (Assess)
- IT corporate governance ensures that shareholder needs, conditions, and options are assessed to determine balanced and agreed-on business objectives. Prioritization and decision-making set the direction to follow. Performance and compliance are measured against the agreed goals.
- IT management plans, builds, executes, and supervises activities in line with the direction set by the governing body to achieve the company's objectives.

- For each objective, information is included on:
  -. High-level information
  A. Processes
  B. Organizational Structure
  C. Information Flows
  D. People, Skills, and Competencies
  E. Policies and Procedures
  F. Culture, Ethics, and Behavior
  G. Services, Infrastructure, and Applications

7.7.- Review exercises

Questions

1. What is COBIT?
2. Who created COBIT and why?
3. What is the objective of COBIT?
4. What are the five domains and the two areas in which the 40 COBIT objectives are organized?
5. What are the parts of a description of a COBIT objective?

Exercises

1. Find a different definition of a COBIT objective than the one shown in this book and describe its parts.
2. Look for a company that is applying COBIT.
3. Explore some of the success stories on the ISACA page and report. You can check the success stories at: https://www.isaca.org/resources/cobit/cobit-case-studies

Chapter 8

Organization of an IT Area

"Governing over many people as if they were few is a matter of dividing them into groups or sectors: it is organization."

Sun Tzu, "The Art of War" Chapter V, Fifth Century BC.

8.1.- Learning objectives

- Appreciate the implications of the place in the organizational chart where the IT area is located.
- Identify the different areas of an IT department.
- Understand the functions of the applications development area of an IT department.
- Understand the roles and responsibilities of the IT operations area in an IT department.
- Understand the role of the administrative activities of the TI area in an organization.
- Recognize the advantages and disadvantages of outsourcing part of the functions of the IT area.
- Analyze the advantages and disadvantages of the decision to centralize or decentralize the operations of the IT area.

8.2.- The functions of an IT area

Different companies assign different functions to the area of information technology. For some, the department is responsible for computer equipment and applications, other companies include telecommunications (including telephony) in the list of responsibilities, and others go so far as to indicate that the definition of the organizational structure of the entire organization is the responsibility of the IT area.

Regardless of the responsibilities assigned to the IT area in each organization, two functions are inalienable: keeping current systems operating and developing new applications. Depending on the size of the company and its dependence on technology, one of the two areas (operation or development) will have predominance in the organizational chart.

Another task that must be part of the IT organizational chart is the management of the IT area. This position is called CIO or Chief Information Officer.

Two critical decisions that define the organizational structure are: centralize or decentralize; and outsourcing or in-house. This chapter discusses the alternatives that exist to organize the IT area in the company.

8.3.- Level in the organization where the IT area is placed

In most companies, there are three places where you can find the IT area in the general organizational chart. The chief technology officer (CIO) may report to the chief executive officer (CEO) and be on the same level as other line directors, such as the chief financial officer (CFO) or the chief operating officer (COO). In other organizations, the technology area is at the Staff level, outside the line of operation of the company, or reports to planning (another area of staff level). However, IT generally reports to the CFO (the finance area) in organizations where IT has been operating for a long time.

Placing the CIO depending on the CEO at the line level shows that technology is essential to the organization. Some companies rely on technology to operate. Imagine a bank without computers or an online store without the Internet. In some companies, the IT area is part of the production line, and the product is highly technological. In those cases, it is common to see two areas of technology, one in charge of production and another providing internal IT services. In a university, for example, it is common to see an area of educational technology (which attends to research processes and classes) and another for administrative technology, which supports the university's operations, finances, and account management.

When the CIO is at the staff level (or reports to a staff area), it usually shows that technology is seen as a need of the organization but not as part of the production process.

In most cases, especially in large companies where the IT area has been around for a long time, it is common to see that IT reports to Finance. One reason may be historical. In many cases, Finance bought the first computer in the organization. Another reason may be that the finance area is also tasked with managing the company's office functions, and the technology area is seen as a support function.

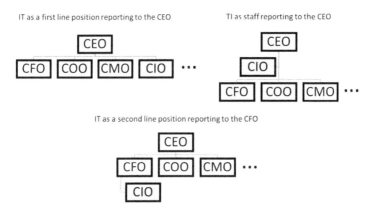

Figure 8.1.- Possible IT locations in the organization

8.4.- Development of new applications

Developing new applications requires the involvement of specialists in systems analysis and design, project management, and software development. If a third-party vendor implements the application, the company still needs someone to oversee the development and handle the relationship with the vendor.

Sometimes analysts specialize by functional area, so it is possible to have analysts for human resource management, purchasing, or production. Other times they form a pool that attacks projects as they are assigned.

A large company can have a systems development manager who coordinates different teams, analysts for each functional area, and developers specializing in each technology used (ERP, databases, Web, etc.)

Mini-case: Technology in a convenience store

How much does a convenience store depend on technology? A cash register is the only technology people see when entering a convenience store. But if they start thinking about the functions of that equipment, they will realize that it is the heart of the operation.

First: the store doesn't just sell milk and bread. It also sells cell phone air time, utility payments, credit card payments, and payments for airline tickets or other purchases made online. 20 to 30 percent of sales in such stores are information processing services (which do not exist physically in the store).

Second: the cash register helps to carry inventory and place refill orders. It is even used to issue merchandise receipts to suppliers who deliver products directly to the store, such as soft drinks or beers.

Third: Few people know, but the cash register is also a training center for the store staff. There they can take online courses and interact with the human resources area.

To answer the initial question: it can be said that a convenience store would have no choice but to close if its cash registers stopped working.

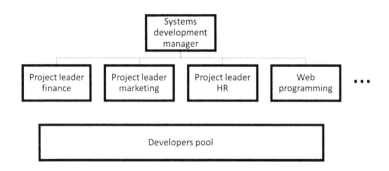

Figure 8.2.- Possible organizational chart of the development area

In a large company, the career of a software specialist will likely begin in the group of developers solving maintenance problems in some application that is in operation. The next step is to specialize in some technology and become an application developer.

With some experience, the developers can become project leaders in charge of a group of developers attending to new projects and then continue as systems analysts.

The next step for an analyst is to specialize in a functional area and then jump to operations or IT management.

8.5.- Support for the operation

During the regular operation of the systems, it is likely that problems will occur or users will have doubts about how to perform some procedure. For these cases, there are help desks (call centers) that are units that respond to users and classify problems. A call center can solve simple problems or direct requests to technical support or systems development areas for more complex issues.

The technical support area comprises specialists in solving technical or configuration problems of system hardware or software. That group also handles equipment maintenance contracts and manages the network. The group can complete some simple equipment or network installations.

A crucial function is that of the head of computer security. This function has two responsibilities: to ensure the continuity of operation (in case of natural disasters or significant failures) and to protect the company in case of computer attacks (including creating a culture of computer security among the staff).

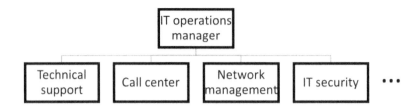

Figure 8.3.- Possible organization chart of the operations area

8.6.- Managing the IT department

As mentioned above, the task of managing the IT function falls to the Chief Information Officer (CIO). This person leads the department, negotiates and manages the budget, and oversees systems planning. Sometimes the CIO has a staff group for systems planning, training, personnel development, and exploring new technologies.

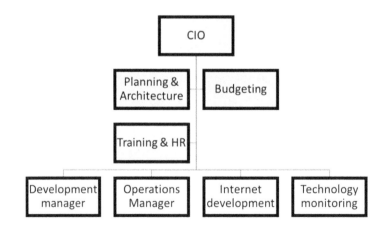

Figure 8.4.- Possible organization chart of the IT area

8.7.- Centralize or decentralize

In the early days of IT in organizations, there was only one computer per company, and the functions had to be centralized. Only the central IT area could acquire equipment and define priorities for IT projects. However, minicomputers soon emerged as inexpensive equipment powerful enough to meet the needs of a small company or department.

With the advent of microcomputers, the computer equipment in the company was no longer a monopoly in the technology area. Any department could buy computers; some departments saw fit to hire staff to operate that equipment and develop their applications. Additionally, end users could create their programs or use commercially available packages. The debate became whether the central area or the user department should manage the equipment.

Among the advantages of centralizing operations are [CIO Source, 2018; Scott, Hill, and Mingay, 2020]:

- Simplifies solution integration
- Better budget control
- Better alignment between the technology platform
- Increased security
- Economies of scale

The main disadvantage is that it can be very bureaucratic and is further away from users and their needs.

Among the advantages of a decentralized operation is [CIO Source, 2018; Scott, Hill, and Mingay, 2020]:

Functional departments have greater control over projects

- Better integration with departmental planning and priorities
- Generally, you get faster results

The most significant disadvantage of decentralization is that sometimes the best solution at the local level is incompatible with other solutions in the organization, leading to integration problems and duplication of efforts.

Most companies have hybrid (federated) models, where certain functions (such as infrastructure, contracting, and help desk) are centralized while others (such as development) are decentralized. [Weill and Ross, 2004]. In general, the recommendation is [Scott, Hill, and Mingay, 2020]:

- Opt for the decentralized structure if the company consists of disparate and disconnected entities.
- Choose a federated structure where there are shared business objectives.
- Look for the centralized (global) structure when there is a unified view of the technology and similar functions throughout the organization.

8.8.- Outsource or in-house

Another critical decision to define the shape and size of an IT area is to determine which functions will be performed with their personnel and which can be outsourced (developed by another company in an outsourcing format).

The advantages of outsourcing are [MJV Team, 2020; Essent, 2021]

- Allows you to focus on critical functions for the company
- Shorter implementation time
- Ease of scaling solutions
- Better budget control
- Access to experienced staff
- Economies of scale

Disadvantages include [Lozhka, 2021; Executech, 2022]

- Less control
- Lower quality
- Possible information leaks
- Negative impact on organizational culture
- Little knowledge of the company by the third party

Any decision will have pros and cons. When choosing an organizational structure, it is essential to define which organization is most likely to meet the company's objectives and execute technology plans at the lowest cost, lower risk, and greater flexibility.

8.9.- Summary

- Organizationally the IT area can be at the line level and report directly to the CEO, be at the staff level, or report to a functional area such as Finance.
- Usually, the IT area is headed by the Chief Information Officer (CIO). It has a group overseeing current operations, another for new developments, and a group in charge of internal administrative functions.
- An important decision is whether to centralize or decentralize functions. The decision depends on the structure and organization of the company.
- Another critical decision is whether to use outsourcing services or perform functions internally. Each alternative has advantages and disadvantages; the final decision will depend on the objectives you want to achieve with the TI area in the organization.

8.10.- Review exercises

Questions

1. What are the different areas of an organizational chart where the IT area can be, and what implications are behind each location?
2. What would be the possible roles in an applications development group?
3. What would be the typical roles in an IT operations group?
4. What are the advantages and disadvantages of centralizing the IT functions?
5. What are the advantages of decentralizing the IT function?
6. What arguments help decide which functions to handle with internal staff and which to use outsourcing?

Exercises

1. Find the organizational chart of a company's TI area, identify the critical decisions made for its design, and explain why those decisions were necessary given the company's context.
2. Find and compare the IT organization chart of one medium-sized and one large company.
3. Look for a bank's IT org chart.
4. Research the IT chart of a retail company.

Chapter 9

Systems Development

"Rushing into manufacturing without being certain of the product is the unrecognized cause of many business failures. People seem to think that the big thing is the factory or the store or the financial backing or the management. The big thing is the product, and any hurry in getting into fabrication before designs are completed is just so much waste time."

Henry Ford, "My Life and Work," 1922

9.1.- Learning objectives

- Describe the life cycle of systems development.
- Identify the advantages and disadvantages of prototype development.
- Recognize the advantages and disadvantages of development by end users.
- Understand the levels of automation.
- Identify critical success factors for an information system development project.
- Appreciate the importance of senior management support in projects.
- Understand the value of supporting operational areas in projects.
- Review the CMMI model, its use, and its maturation phases.

9.2.- The systems development life cycle

Once the IT planning process is complete, the next step is to put it into practice. A plan without execution is just a dream. However, implementing IT solutions takes a lot of work. It requires the interaction of users, analysts, programmers, and hardware specialists. Factors such as the complexity of the problem, the available time, technology, and budget help determine the best methodology to follow in developing the new system.

A technique for creating and implementing an information system is known as the Software Development Life Cycle (SDLC). Figure 9. 1 illustrates the steps of the process [Kendall & Kendall, 2005; Laudon & Laudon, 2019].

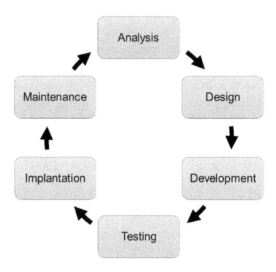

Figure 9.1 – System Development Lifecycle Phases (SDLC)

The phases of the software development life cycle are as follows:

Analysis: Defines what to do

Design: Answers the question of how the system will operate

Development: Ensures that the software specified in the previous two phases is purchased, rented, or built

Testing: Verifies that the system components (people, hardware, and software) perform well together and with the expected workloads.

Implementation: Sets the new system in operation in the organization and manages the change from the old way of doing things to the new.

Maintenance: Ensures that the system continues to operate and provides the required information, correcting errors and reacting to changes in requirements

Each of the identified phases is then broken down.

Analysis

This phase aims to define what the new system should do. Do not worry about how to do it (that's the next phase). Concentrate on the required information, who needs it, and what will be done.

Design

The previous step defined what to do; this phase focuses on who produces the information, how it is processed, what products are generated, and the flow of process data. The question in this phase is: "how is the system going to work?". You must define the components and how they will interact with each other. The design documentation must be detailed enough to build the complete system in the next stage.

Development

The first activity at this stage is to see if a program is available in the market that works or can be adjusted to our needs. If a suitable product exists, it is bought or rented; if it does not exist, it must be developed. The software must be running error-free before moving on to the next stage.

In some cases, as with enterprise systems (ERP), it is possible to buy a solution (or part of it) and configure it or adapt it to meet the company's needs.

If the design has sufficient detail, it is possible to send the specifications to external software factories, where programmers develop the requested applications. A software factory can be located anywhere in the world, preferring places where trained personnel are available and willing to work for a lower wage. This practice is known as outsourcing.

Testing

Even if each piece of software works, it is critical to test the entire system, that is, operate the process from where the information originates to where the results are generated. All components (human and mechanical) must work properly and interact without a problem.

It is also essential to test with typical workloads. Sometimes the software works very well with one or two transactions, but if the operation requires hundreds or thousands of transactions, it is vital to ensure that the system will support real-life environments.

Implementation

The next phase is to put the designed system into operation. The new system represents a change. In most cases, a system replaces an old way of doing things. At this stage, it is essential to train the personnel using the new system and plan to transition from the old one to the new one.

There are three main ways to make the transition: it can be done in one step (one day, the old system is turned off, and the new one is turned on). This option is economical because it requires little expense in the transition but is very risky. If the new system does not work or presents problems, this would cause a disaster.

The second way is to run the two systems, the old and the new, in parallel for a while. This option is safe because the old system is only turned off if the new one proves that it works. But it is costly as it requires twice as much work for a while.

The third alternative is a phased implementation. If the system can be separated into parts, it is possible to implement a module in one department and then move on with the others. With the first module in place, you can install the next one, and so on, until the complete system is installed.

Maintenance

A computer can break down, or a disk can be damaged, which requires maintenance. But what does it mean to maintain a process or a computer program? Programs always do the same thing; they usually don't modify themselves. Maintenance of software and processes involves two activities: correcting errors not detected in the testing phase; and ensuring that the system complies with providing relevant, complete, and timely information. That is, ensuring that the system is still helpful for making decisions.

Valuable information from yesterday may be less useful today. The problem is that the decisions that a system supports happen in the real world, and the world changes. The system must be modified so that it continues to provide the needed information given the changing conditions of the environment where the decisions it supports exist. Another type of change is when the requirements of the process change, such as when a new tax appears, or interest rates change.

Eventually, conditions change too much, or new opportunities arise, leading to a requirement for a new information system and a restart of the cycle.

9.3.- Development by prototypes

The systems development lifecycle requires user needs to be identified and defined before moving on to the development stages. This methodology works well for large systems with high levels of complexity, as it helps to divide a problem into parts and identify possible solutions. However, the process takes a lot of time and requires that the issue be well understood before starting the development of solutions.

In the decision-making environment, some decisions that require support come unexpectedly and must be made quickly (which would make it unfeasible to follow a complete development methodology). On the other hand, some problems are so unique that it is difficult to know what it takes to solve them in advance.

If a person wants to buy a suit, the most common solution is to go to a store and try on some models until the person finds the right fit. It is uncommon to go to a store with a list of specifications of what one wants. A similar phenomenon can occur with software. If it's hard for users to know what they need, they may want to try different models until the right solution is found.

The technique used in these cases is called prototyping. Prototype design consists of quickly and inexpensively building an experimental system to evaluate the required functionality [Laudon & Laudon, 2019]. It doesn't have to be a functional system; it can be just a series of images of what would be seen on the screen so the user can feel the proposed functionality.

The process is iterative. The prototype is designed and tested; corrections are made and resubmitted. The process is repeated until an acceptable version is found.

Once the process is complete, if the prototype works, it can be stabilized, documented, and delivered to the end user. The other alternative is to use the prototype as the specification of the desired system, which is then built, tested, and implemented.

9.4.- Development by end users

Some types of systems can be built directly by end users using macros in Excel or designing dashboards in Tableau, for example. A positive outcome is that the users easily accept these systems. The problem is that not being built with formal processes, it is typical for systems designed by an end user to have failures, be unable to process large volumes of information, or be valid only for a particular person or decision.

A possible danger is that systems designed by end users may not have contingency plans in case data is lost. If the company will depend on applications developed by end users, it is convenient to work on using those systems as prototypes and build a formal system based on the design.

An acceptable compromise is to establish specific hardware, software, or data standards for all end-user systems used in the organization. Combining this with awareness of information security and risk prevention processes is essential.

9.5.- Automation or redesign of processes

A new information system brings changes to the organization. Sometimes the changes are simple. We look for a way to do the same thing that is already done but more efficiently. The technique is called automation.

When automating, it is possible that new bottlenecks are found in the processes or that other problems with the current approaches are discovered. The situation requires a complete review of how things are done, eliminating steps that do not add value and changing others. This approach is called rationalization.

The automation and rationalization of processes make the current approach more efficient. However, there comes the point where the only way to speed up a process further and maximize the potential of the technology is to rethink the activities from the start. This technique is known as business process reengineering. The term was coined by Michael Hammer [Hammer, 1990] and consisted of changing the focus to solve a problem.

Hammer illustrates the idea of reengineering with an analogy. He says that instead of paving dirt roads so you can go faster, it's better to rethink the route and look for better ways to get the expected results. The question is not how I get along the road faster but why I want to get to that destination. Perhaps the answer will show that a phone call would be enough instead of a new route. Maybe the answer is that we can build a bridge that eliminates much of the trajectory.

The main idea of identifying transformational projects is to change the question. Refocus the effort from how I do this faster to why I do this, or could I do something else? Not all projects require reengineering. These are riskier, time-consuming, face more significant resistance to change, and are more complicated than an automation project. However, in some instances, rethinking processes may be the only solution to a problem in an organization.

9.6.- Critical success factors for a new information system

For a system to be successful, it must work well, but more important is that it is used correctly for the people and functions intended.

Building a new information system is a process that requires a lot of effort and the participation of personnel from different areas. If you plan to develop an application to support the sales process, sales personnel must participate in the analysis and design of the solution. This approach requires getting some salespeople out of their sales work to support creating a new system.

If the sales managers are not interested in the project and assign their worst salesperson to the task, the resulting system might not work as required. Access to the best salespersons is necessary, probably distracting them from work for a while, so their ideas can help generate an excellent new solution.

Building a successful application requires the participation of areas that would be the system's users. In turn, they will need senior management's support to accept a drop in productivity (which could result if the best employees are taken out of their jobs for a while to help with the new system).

From the earliest software development projects, it was clear that these projects had special rules [Brooks, 1972]. Top management support and user involvement are critical success factors in developing new information systems.

Among the factors that have proven to be essential for the success of a system's development are:

- Support from senior management
- User Engagement
- The professionalism of the development staff
- The proper budget and time
- Clarity in objectives
- Risk management and
- Application of best practices in development

9.7.- The CMM and CMMI model

Several tools and methodologies exist for systems analysis and design and software engineering. One of the most widely used is CMM (Capability Maturity Model) and a CMMI (Capability Maturity Model Integration) extension [Humphrey, 1988].

CMMI consists of best practices that address development activities applied to products and services. It addresses techniques that cover the product lifecycle from conception to delivery and maintenance. Organizations from many industries, including aerospace, banking, hardware manufacturers, software, defense, automobile manufacturing, and telecommunications, use CMMI [Chaudhari, 2016]

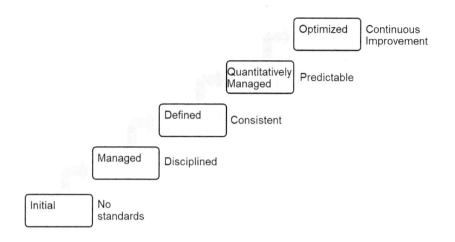

Figure 9.2.- CMMI maturation levels

The CMMI model provides numerous guides for assessing an organization's maturity and the improvements needed in various process areas to move from one level to the next. [Gefen and Zviran, 2006; Lankhorst, 2009]. There are five levels of maturity, as shown in Figure 9.2. The detail of each one is described in Figure 9.3.

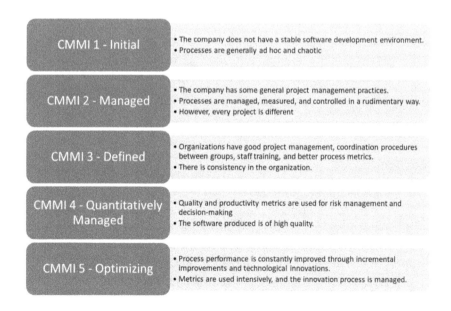

Figure 9.3.- Detail of the different maturity levels of CMMI

9.8.- Summary

- A technique for creating and implementing an information system is known as the Software Development Life Cycle (SDLC).
- The phases of the software development lifecycle are: analysis, design, development, testing, implementation, and maintenance.
- Another technique available is prototyping, where a rapid system is designed that serves as a sample and goes through an iterative review process. At the end of the process, depending on the type of prototype manufactured, the prototype can be the final product, or it can become the specifications for the formal construction of a complete system.
- End users can develop their applications. It is essential to be careful that these applications follow security protocols to prevent the company from relying for its operation on unstable or unsupported systems.
- The support of senior management and users' participation is essential for the success of a new system.
- CMMI is a standard that consists of best practices that address development activities applied to products and services. It addresses techniques covering the product lifecycle from conception to delivery and maintenance, ranking companies into five maturity levels.
- The CMMI model provides numerous guides for assessing an organization's maturity and the improvements needed in various process areas to move from one level to the next.

9.9.- Review exercises

Questions

1. What is the systems development lifecycle?
2. What are the steps in the systems development lifecycle?
3. What stage of the life cycle describes what the new system will do?
4. What is the difference between automating and reengineering?
5. What is the product of the design phase of a system?
6. What is tested during the testing stage of a system?
7. What are the three ways to implement a system, and what are the advantages and disadvantages of each one?
8. Why is it essential to give maintenance to a system?
9. What is a prototype design, and when is it convenient to use?

10. What advantages and problems can end-user application development present?
11. Why is it critical to have the support of senior management when carrying out an information technology project?
12. What is the CMMI model, and what is its objective?
13. What are the maturation levels of CMMI?

Exercises

1. Interview the technology manager at a company, ask them to remember a successful project, and ask if any of the critical factors mentioned in this chapter occurred.
2. Interview the technology manager at a company, and ask if they remember a project that has failed and what caused the failure.
3. Describe a business process reengineering project.
4. Identify and describe an automation project
5. Look for a company that has used the CMMI model.

Part IV

IT Implementation

Chapter 10

IT Service Management

"The most dangerous phrase a DP manager can use is 'We've always done it that way.' "

Grace Murray Hopper, Computerworld report, 1976, [Surden, 1976].

10.1.- Learning objectives

- Describe an IT service is and its characteristics.
- Recognize the different categories of services.
- Understand the definition and value of ITIL.
- Recognize the critical disciplines of ITIL V2.
- Recognize the service lifecycle.
- Know the service value chain.
- Identify the different roles involved in ITIL and their functions.
- Know how to use the ITIL guidelines.

10.2.- Delivery of services

Organizations provide services (referring to products or services) for customers. The services are the product of the company's business processes. Customers receive a benefit from the services (so they are willing to pay for them) and do not manage the operations or costs of the company; they only receive the final product.

The organization's business processes require applications, information, and processing. From the IT perspective, the business process is the customer, IT is the supplier, and the services are the applications, information, or processing provided.

According to Gartner, IT services apply technical and business insights to enable organizations to create, manage, and optimize or access information and business processes [Gartner, 2023].

An IT service must meet two characteristics [Hertvik, 2019].

1. It must produce something that the customer values.
2. The customer should refrain from managing the costs or risks of the service. Services are designed, implemented, enhanced, and retired by IT.

There are different categories of services: Business process services, application services, and infrastructure services [Gartner, 2023].

- **Business Process Services:** Complete repeatable activities to obtain concrete results for the client. Business services usually have a start and end point and a well-defined process. These services include payroll processing, capturing orders, updating customer information, etc.
- **Application Services:** Develop, install, configure, migrate, update, support, and secure access to all applications. It also includes load balancing, performance monitoring, and needs analysis to operate applications optimally.
- **Infrastructure Services:** Build, configure, and maintain hardware components, networks, servers, communications lines, firewalls, etc., that are required to access applications or other services.

10.3.- ITIL, a compilation of best practices for service delivery

To improve service delivery in the UK central government, the UK Office of Government Commerce (OGC) designed a series of documents compiling best practices in IT service delivery. The compilation is called ITIL (IT Infrastructure Library). The goal was to create a comprehensive and consistent record of best practices while helping the private sector develop consulting techniques and tools to support ITIL [Lankhorst, 2009].

Since its launch, ITIL has evolved. As of 2013, ITIL is owned by AXELOS, a co-investment between the UK Cabinet Office and Capita (the UK's most extensive business process outsourcing and professional services company).

ITIL V2 was organized around two key disciplines:

- **Service support:** help desk, incident report, change, release, and configuration.
- **Service delivery:** service level, capacity, availability, contingency planning, and financial management.

ITIL V3 presents the concept of the service lifecycle and is organized into five areas:

- Service Strategy
- Service Design
- Service Transition
- Service Operation
- Continuous service improvement

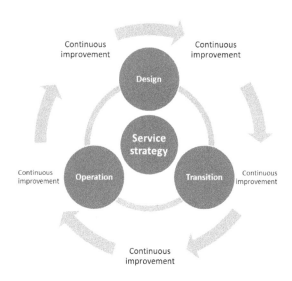

Figure 10.1.- ITIL V3 Service Lifecycle

In 2019 ITIL V4 was introduced, replacing the service lifecycle with the service value chain consisting of six stages [Anand 2019]:

- **Engage:** Interact with external stakeholders to foster good understanding.
- **Plan:** Create an understanding of the vision, status, and directions for improving products and services.
- **Improve:** Ensure the continuous improvement of products, services, and practices throughout the value chain.
- **Design and transition:** Ensure that products and services consistently meet quality, cost, and delivery time expectations.
- **Obtain/Build:** Ensure that products and services are available when and where they are needed, meeting specifications.
- **Deliver and support:** Ensure that products and services are delivered and supported to specifications.

ITIL V4 does not invalidate ITIL V3. While V3 focuses on how to deliver service, V4 focuses on how to create value.

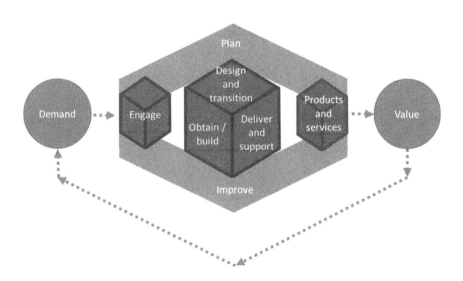

Figure 10. 2.- Value chain of the ITIL V4 service. Source Anand [2019]

10.4.- Roles involved in ITIL

In ITIL, there are several generic roles, such as Service Owner, as well as more specific roles, such as Service Desk Analyst, which are required for particular stages of the process lifecycle [AXELOS, 2023; Aguter, 2012]:

Process owner: Responsible for a process to work well and do what it should do. It must be just one person to avoid contradictions. Among their responsibilities are the following:

- Define strategies, policies, and process standards
- Support in the design
- Make sure the process is documented
- Audit the process

Process Manager: Responsible for managing the operation of a process. There may be more than one (for example, one PM for each business unit). Among his responsibilities are the following:

- Ensure that the activities of a process are done
- Assign people to roles and manage resources
- Monitor and report process performance
- Identify areas of opportunity

Process Practitioner: The role can be combined with that of a process administrator. It is responsible for the following:

- Perform process activities
- Understand how your activities create value
- Interact with other participants in the process
- Make sure the inputs and outputs are correct

Service Owner: Is responsible for the delivery of IT services to the customer. It does not necessarily execute the process activities but ensures the work is completed. Its activities include:

- Responsible to the customer for the start, transition, maintenance, and support of the service
- Accountable to the IT director for the delivery of the service
- Communicate with the customer about the service
- Serve as a problem escalation point
- Participate in Service Level Negotiations (SLAs)

The model used to define the work of each role is that of RACI (Responsible, Accountable, Consulted, Informed).

INV IT staff involved in service delivery need to understand business priorities and how the technology area supports them. Additional skills required include:

- Administrative skills
- Know how to manage meetings
- Communication skills (oral and written)
- Negotiation skills
- Analytical thinking

10.5.- Sample checklists for SLA OLA

An example of an ITIL process is the SLA or Service Level Agreement. An SLA is an agreement between the IT services area and the customer. OLA Operating Level Agreement is an agreement between the service area and another part of the same organization dealing with the delivery of infrastructure services. This section cites a checklist based on process map information [Kempter, 2021].

The idea of a template is that when it is necessary to define an SLA, no time is wasted creating new formats or researching what information to include. ITIL already shows a guide that can be used to design the forms and ensure that every detail is remembered. Like this, there are other formats for the different components of IT services.

Checklist, SLA OLA

ITIL Processes: ITIL Service Design – Service Level Management

"Service name

Clearance information (with location and date)

1. Service Level Manager
2. Customer representative

Contract duration

1. Start and end dates
2. Rules regarding renewal and termination of the agreement (if applicable, also rules regarding early termination of the agreement)

Description/ desired customer outcome

1. Business justification and benefits
2. Business processes/ activities on the customer side supported by the service
3. Desired outcome in terms of utility (example: "Field staff can access enterprise applications xxx and yyy without being constrained by location or time")
4. Desired outcome in terms of warranty (example: "High availability required during office hours in locations ...")

Communication between customer and service provider

1. Responsible contact person on customer side with contact details
2. Designated Business Relationship Manager on service provider side with contact details
3. Service Reporting (contents and intervals of service reports to be produced by the service provider)
4. Procedure for handling exceptions and complaints (e.g. details to be included in formal complaints, agreed response times, escalation procedure)
5. Satisfaction surveys (description of the procedure for measuring customer satisfaction on a regular basis)
6. Service Reviews (description of the procedure for reviewing the service with the customer on a regular basis)

Service and asset criticality

1. Identification of business-critical assets connected with the service
   a. Vital Business Functions (VBFs) supported by the service
   b. Other critical assets used within the service (e.g. certain types of business data)
2. Estimation of the business impact caused by a loss of the service or assets (in monetary terms, or using a classification scheme)

Service times

1. Times when the service is required to be available
2. Exceptions (e.g. weekends, public holidays)

Required types and levels of support

1. On-site support
   a. Area/ locations
   b. Types of users
   c. Types of infrastructure to be supported
   d. Reaction and resolution times (according to priorities, definition of priorities e.g. for the classification of Incidents)
2. Remote support
   a. Area/ locations
   b. Types of users (user groups granted access to the service)
   c. Types of infrastructure to be supported
   d. Reaction and resolution times (according to priorities, definition of priorities e.g. for the classification of Incidents)

Service level requirements/ targets

1. Availability targets and commitments
   a. Conditions under which the service is considered to be unavailable (e.g. if the service is offered at several locations)
   b. Availability targets (exact definition of how the agreed availability levels will be calculated, based on agreed service time and downtime)
   c. Reliability targets (required by some customers, usually defined as MTBF (Mean Time Between Failures) or MTBSI (Mean Time Between Service Incidents))
   d. Maintainability targets (required by some customers, usually defined as MTRS (Mean Time to Restore Service))
   e. Down times for maintenance (number of allowed down times, pre-notification periods)
   f. Restrictions on maintenance, e.g. allowed maintenance windows, seasonal restrictions on maintenance, and procedures to announce planned service interruptions
   g. Definitions of Major Incidents as well as Emergency Changes and Releases to resolve urgent issues, including procedures to announce unplanned service interruptions
   h. Requirements regarding availability reporting
2. Capacity/ performance targets and commitments
   a. Required capacity (lower/upper limit) for the service, e.g.
      i. Numbers and types of transactions
      ii. Numbers and types of users

        iii. Business cycles (daily, weekly) and seasonal variations
   b. Response times from applications
   c. Requirements for scalability (assumptions for the medium and long-term increase in workload and service utilization)
   d. Requirements regarding capacity and performance reporting
3. Service Continuity commitments (availability of the service in the event of a disaster)
   a. Time within which a defined level of service must be re-established
   b. Time within which normal service levels must be restored

Technical standards/ specification of the service interface

Mandated technical standards and specification of the technical service interface

Responsibilities

1. Duties of the service provider
2. Duties of the customer (contract partner for the service)
3. Responsibilities of service users (e.g. with respect to IT security)
4. IT Security aspects to be observed when using the service (if applicable, references to relevant IT Security Policies)

Pricing model

1. Cost for the service provision
2. Rules for penalties/ charge backs

Change history

List of annexes and references (if applicable)

Glossary (if applicable)"

10.6.- Success stories

Axelos has a page describing success stories of the use of ITIL in different markets and organizations. The information can be found at: https://www.axelos.com/resource-hub/case-study

Some examples are listed below:

Mini-case: Bimbo Group

Bimbo Group is a winner of the ITIL Experience Award [Gutierrez, 2018]. The company used ITIL to integrate and coordinate service management across its global sites. ITIL allows services to be standardized worldwide. The company managed to decentralize its IT services from Mexico to each country, changed the conversation from tickets to services, and promoted separate repositories of information by region. More information can be found on the following page: https://www.axelos.com/resource-hub/case-study/grupo-bimbo-winning-the-itil-experience-award

---

Mini-Case: Pittsburgh City Government

Pittsburgh City Government [Axelos 2021]: Pennsylvania's second-largest city had issues with the quality of IT services it provided to different departments. After adopting ITIL and starting a massive training program for their staff, they managed, among other things: to create formats so that each department could manage its website directly, optimize the routes of its staff to update computer equipment throughout the administration, respond to the demands for equipment and services that arose from the response to the COVID-19 emergency. More information can be found on the following page: https://www.axelos.com/resource-hub/case-study/pittsburgh-itil-better-public-service-provision

---

Spotify [Källgården, 2019]: The company's IT team faced four challenges:

- Visualizing the total workload
- Managing the workload
- Coordinating the needs of internal customers
- Managing different types of work

Using ITIL, they managed to bring order to the demands for services in the IT area. They realized that ITIL is based on best practices and common sense. Processes exist to support the organization in achieving its goals. More information can be found on the following page: https://www.axelos.com/resource-hub/case-study/spotify-itil-case-study

10.7.- Summary

- IT services refer to the application of technical and business knowledge to enable organizations to create, manage, and optimize or access information and business processes.
- An IT service must meet two characteristics:
  - It must produce something that the customer values.
  - The customer should refrain from managing the costs or risks of the service. Services are designed, implemented, enhanced, and retired by IT.
- ITIL (IT Infrastructure Library) is a series of documents compiling best practices in delivering IT services.
- ITIL has evolved from contemplating two critical disciplines, defining the service lifecycle, to the service value chain.
- In ITIL, there are several generic roles, such as Service Owner, and more specific functions, such as Service Desk Analyst, which are required for particular stages of the process lifecycle.
- There are also templates or guides for each type of service.

10.8.- Review exercises

Questions

1. What is an IT service?
2. What are the characteristics of an IT service?
3. What are the different categories of services?
4. What is ITIL, and how was it created?
5. What are the two key disciplines of ITIL V2?
6. What is the service lifecycle?
7. What is the difference between the service lifecycle and the service value chain?
8. List the roles available in ITIL and describe their functions.

Exercises

1. Find the template for an ITIL service and discuss its relevance in a real application.
2. Find an organization that is using ITIL and describe its results.
3. Describe the problem situation and results of one of the success stories published by Axelos in: https://www.axelos.com/resource-hub/case-study

Chapter 11

Technology Infrastructure

"But if these machines were ingenious, what shall we think of the calculating machine of Mr. Babbage? What shall we think of an engine of wood and metal which can not only compute astronomical and navigation tables to any given extent, but render the exactitude of its operations mathematically certain through its power of correcting its possible errors? What shall we think of a machine which can not only accomplish all this, but actually print off its elaborate results, when obtained, without the slightest intervention of the intellect of man?"

Edgar Allan Poe, Maelzel's Chess-Player, 1836.

11.1.- Learning objectives

- Identify the components of a technology platform.
- Describe the parts and operation of the hardware platform.
- Describe the functions of an operating system.
- Explain how application software operates.
- Understand the three key technologies that support the Internet.
- Describe the advantages and disadvantages of cloud computing.

11.2.- Components of a technology infrastructure

Technology infrastructure, the platform necessary for a business intelligence application to operate, refers to much more than just a computer.

A computer (hardware) alone is useless. It needs a series of programs with instructions on interpreting keystrokes, moving information to and from memory, and displaying results on a screen (to name a few). Those instructions show the computer how to operate and are the operating system.

Solving real problems (such as Business Intelligence) requires specialized application programs that run on top of the operating system. They include the procedures and calculations needed to convert data into useful information.

Data might come from more than one place. Sometimes it is stored on different computers. Therefore, application programs also need communication between computers, sometimes through the Internet.

Technology infrastructure refers to the hardware, operating systems, applications, and communication programs that turn data into useful information. Figure 11.1 shows an outline of the components of a technology platform.

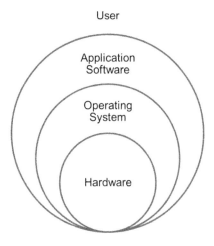

Figure 11.1 – Components of a technology platform

11.3.- Hardware platforms

Hardware is the computer equipment where information is processed. A computer has several components: input and output equipment, processing units, memory, and secondary storage. Figure 11. 2 shows a general outline of a computer.

Input units enter information into the computer. The most common examples are a keyboard, mouse, camera, and microphone. Some computers may also have touch-sensitive screens or fingerprint readers. Other input equipment might be scanners, barcode readers, or magnetic stripe readers.

Output units are how we get information out of the computer. The most common output units are displays and printers. Other typical output units are the speakers with which the computer can send signals (beeps) or even play some audio. More specialized output units can be robots with movement or vibrators (to indicate on a handheld device that the information has been received).

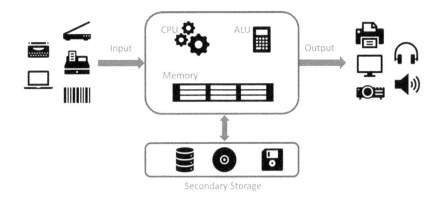

Figure 11.2 - General layout of a computer

Inside the processing unit are three main components: The Central Processing Unit or CPU, the arithmetic logic unit or ALU, and the main memory. The CPU is the part that controls the movement of information among components, instructs the ALU to perform some operation, or tells the memory where to store a value. The ALU performs mathematical functions or comparisons between two numbers provided by the CPU, returning the result. Main memory is where the data and programs running on the computer are stored.

A computer program is a series of instructions stored in the computer's memory. The CPU takes the first instruction and executes it, then moves on to the next until the program ends.

Since, in many computers, the main memory requires power to operate, sometimes it is necessary to store data outside the computer on secondary storage units such as disks, tapes, or USB sticks (to avoid having to reenter the programs every time the computer is powered on). When activated, most computers have instructions for downloading the operating system programs from secondary storage to main memory so that they can start operations.

Physical size, processing speed, and memory capacity are essential to define the speed of a computer. Electricity has to travel from one component of the computer to the next. Smaller computers take less time to move data around. Memory is crucial because moving information within memory is faster than bringing it from external devices. A machine with limited memory has to wait to bring in data from secondary storage drives to keep operating.

The top microcomputer manufacturers are Dell, HP, Apple, Acer, and Lenovo. IBM, Hitachi, and Unisys manufacture more powerful mainframe computers for large enterprises or complex operations.

11.4.- Operating systems

As explained earlier, hardware alone is useless. It needs programing to be able to send something to print or display it on the screen. Those instructions are called the operating system. There are some standard operating systems designed for different computer hardware. To print something, you have to give the order to the operating system, which will send the correct commands for the hardware in use.

The most common operating systems for PCs are Windows and Mac OS X. In medium and large computers, there are operating systems such as Unix or Linux. Small devices, such as phones or tablets, usually use Android, iOS, Windows phone OS, or Symbian.

The advantage of standard operating systems is that if a program runs on Windows, nothing needs to be changed if the operating system runs on a Dell computer or an HP machine.

11.5.- Application software

Application software runs on top of the operating system. These are the computer programs that process information. Examples include business applications such as SAP, ORACLE, or Microsoft Dynamics; tailor-made systems such as payroll or inventory; database platforms; and packages such as Word, Excel, or Tableau.

The user works with the application software and usually does not have to worry if they change the computer or even the operating system.

11.6.- Internet

A computer can work with the information it has in its main memory and what it can access from its secondary storage. Sometimes it is necessary to bring data from other computers in the same office or the other side of the world. The data comes via computer networks, connections between computers that allow them to exchange information. The most prevalent network today is the Internet.

The Internet is a communications architecture that allows different computer networks worldwide to interact with each other. The Internet emerged in the United States in the 1970s but became popular in the mid-1990s. By 2020, more than half of the earth's population had access to the Internet [Kahn & Dennis, 2022].

The Internet is based on three key technologies [Laudon & Traver, 2018]:

- Packet switching
- TCP/IP Communications Protocol
- Client-server communications architecture.

Packet switching is a method of dividing messages into smaller units called packets. Each packet includes identifying information that describes the type of information it contains, what part of the message it is, where it comes from, and its destination.

Each packet may follow a different route. Upon arrival at the destination, the packages are reassembled, and the original message is completed on the receiving computer.

Figure 11.3 shows how packet switching consists of each node sending each packet to the next computer on the network toward the recipient's address. In turn, the computer receiving the message forwards it to the next available computer in the right direction until the packet reaches its destination. If a route is busy or a node is not responding, the message is sent by an alternate route. Eventually, all packages arrive at the destination computer; the target computer acknowledges the packet's arrival and reassembles the entire message from its parts. If the source computer doesn't get a receipt stating that all the packages arrived correctly, it simply sends a replacement package.

Figure 11.3 illustrate the military origins of the Internet network. If a node were to be disabled for any reason, the network would not stop working because there are many ways to get the information to its destination. Therefore, when there is a problem or natural disaster in a city, and it cannot transmit data, the network does not stop. The messages that naturally follow that path use another route without requiring users or administrators to do anything special.

However, this advantage has also become a problem. Just as a natural disaster cannot stop the Internet, neither can a decree of some government institution. Users usually find ways to circumvent any barrier that is placed. There are documented cases of popular revolts, coordinated from the Internet, that governments cannot easily control. One example occurred in the spring of 2011 when protests in different Arab countries culminated in overthrowing several local governments. The event is known as the Arab Spring [History, 2020].

Fake news is another problem exacerbated by the Internet. Since there is no central authority, it is almost impossible to delete messages, even if they contain intentionally erroneous information. In the same way, if someone uploads an offensive photograph, it is nearly impossible to remove it from the network.

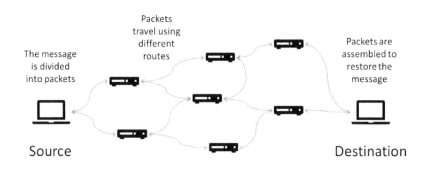

Figure 11.3 – Packet switching

The second key element that supports the Internet is the TCP/IP (Transmission Control Protocol/Internet Protocol) communications protocol. This standard establishes the packet addressing scheme, the way sending and receiving computers are connected, and the way the message is separated into packets on the sending computer and the packets are reassembled on the receiving computer.

The third element: the client-server communications architecture, is a computing model where one computer (the client) connects with another (the server) to ask for information, minimizing the amount of data transmitted using communication networks. The data processing happens on the server. The only information that travels through the web is the client's request and the page with the response. In this way, there is no need to send the complete contents of a database to answer a client's request, making communications faster.

For example, if you enter the Google page and type the phrase "Digital Transformation," Google will respond with a message stating that there are about 80 million results, followed by the first ten results of its list. What has happened is that the request traveled to Google's computers. Google's server searched their data and responded by sending only the first names in its list. This information can be sent quickly to the client's computer because only one phrase travels one way, and a page travels back through the network. The rest of the almost 80 million responses are only sent if they are requested. The user can request page two or three, and Google will respond with them.

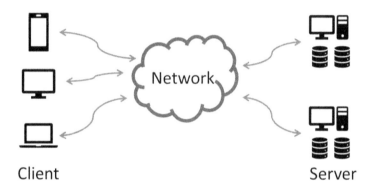

Client   Server

Figure 11.4 – Client-server architecture

The client-server communications architecture results in the network responding quickly and can be used with any client computer, even if these are not necessarily very powerful. That allows personal computers, tablets, phones, and even kitchen appliances to interact with the network without requiring expensive processors, a lot of memory, or large storage capacity.

Many other protocols and programs support the Internet, such as HTTP, SMTP, and FTP protocols, as well as software applications.

Minicase: "Fake news" and its political influence

False news reports that appear with the emergence of social networks, also known as "fake news," consists of stories that seem to be accurate reports but have no support or reliable sources.

Fake news creates "competing versions of information and the truth" and is designed and broadcast to deceive or manipulate people; or for economic or political gain. However, the term has also been used to discredit accurate news or contrary opinions.

The challenge of fake news is discussed in an interview published by the United Nations [Dickinson, 2018]. You can find the full interview here: https://news.un.org/en/audio/2018/05/1008682

11.7.- Cloud computing

An example of client-server architecture mentioned in the previous section is what is known as cloud computing, where computing and storage power resides in large data servers. The user can access these from almost anywhere without needing sophisticated devices as a client.

The advantage of cloud computing is that it can serve users almost immediately. Once an application is placed in the cloud, adding a new office is a matter of connecting the office to the Internet. Once connected, the office can access the full power of the application without investing in expensive equipment or modifying facilities. Another advantage when applications are shared among many users is that the cost of creating and operating cloud solutions is distributed among many participants so that it can become quite economical.

One disadvantage of cloud solutions is that the operation depends on a data connection. If the link were to fail, there would be no access to any information. Another disadvantage cited by some users is that data that may be confidential is moved on public networks, so it is vital to measure the security levels of these applications before committing to use them.

Minicase – Salesforce, a complete CRM system installed in 15 minutes

Salesforce.com, Inc. is a San Francisco-based company that builds and operates a cloud CRM platform. Customers can hire their services and run a complete CRM solution for their company paying only a monthly rent for each user they want to access the platform.

A complete CRM solution for a medium to small business could cost tens of thousands of dollars and require a year to implement. Using Salesforce takes little time to boot, requires no additional hardware to a PC and an Internet connection, and could cost between $50 and $200 per month, depending on the number of people that need to access the information. You can watch videos explaining how the platform works on the company's web page on Salesforce.com

11.8.- Summary

- Technology infrastructure refers to the hardware, operating systems, applications, and communication programs that turn data into useful information
- Hardware alone is useless. It needs programing to be able to send something to print or display it on the screen. Those instructions are called the operating system.
- Application software runs on top of the operating system. These are the computer programs that process information
- The Internet is a communications architecture that allows different computer networks worldwide to interact with each other.
- Internet is based on three key technologies: packet switching, TCP/IP communications protocol, and client-server communications architecture.
- Cloud computing is a variant of the client-server model where computing and storage power resides in large data servers. The user can access these from almost anywhere without needing sophisticated devices as a client.

11.9.- Review exercises

Questions

1. What are the components of a technology architecture?
2. What is hardware?
3. What are the main parts of a computer?
4. What does an operating system do?
5. Mention some examples of operating systems
6. Mention some examples of software applications
7. What are the three key technologies of the Internet?
8. What are the advantages of cloud computing?
9. What are the disadvantages of cloud computing?

Exercises

1. Identify the input units of a computer.
2. List at least five output units of a computer.
3. Find four hardware vendors.
4. Identify two different brands of computers that use the same operating system.
5. Find information about cloud-based ERP solution providers.

Chapter 12

Technology Provider Management

> *"Every individual necessarily labours to render the annual revenue of the society as great as he can. He generally, indeed, neither intends to promote the public interest, nor knows how much he is promoting it. ... he intends only his own gain, and he is in this, as in many other eases, led by an invisible hand to promote an end which was no part of his intention, nor is it always the worse for the society that it was no part of it. By pursuing his own interest, he frequently promotes that of the society more effectually than when he really intends to promote it."*

Adam Smith, "The Wealth of Nations" 1776.

.

12.1.- Learning objectives

- Identify the phases of the procurement process.
- Define the activities that occur during the need recognition phase.
- Explain how a contract is formalized.
- Understand how a public bidding process works.
- Identify the responsibilities of the parties during the execution of a contract.
- Recognize the importance and process of change control.
- Identify a technological partner's roles in defining, developing, and operating projects.
- Appreciate the value of treating colleagues with respect and honesty.

12.2.- The phases of the technology purchase process

The amount organizations spend on computer applications and information technology purchases is a significant part of the company's total operating budget. At the same time, the computer equipment and solutions market can be highly lucrative for specialized organizations. Understanding the technology purchase process is critical for sellers and buyers.

Many believe that a purchase starts when a buyer sends a request for proposal (RFP) to potential suppliers; however, the actual process begins much earlier. The specifications of the solutions to buy start with the identification of a business need. The complete procurement process consists of three stages [Alanís, 2020]:

- Recognition of the need
- Formalization of the contract
- Contract Administration

The first phase, recognition of the need, starts with identifying and defining the company's needs. Designing a good solution requires an understanding of existing and emerging technologies. Preparing a detailed RFP that would attract possible suppliers at reasonable prices involves experience.

The second phase, the contract's formalization, is generally a very rigid process handled by areas specialized in negotiation or acquisitions. Depending on the investment required and the company's policies, the purchase can be awarded directly to a specific supplier, require two or more quotes from different suppliers, or even need a public bidding process. Public bidding is a ceremony widely used in government organizations, where suppliers deliver their offers in a sealed envelope. All bids are publicly opened and analyzed to select a winner.

Once a winner has been chosen, the contract is formalized and executed. During the execution phase, the project is developed. It is essential to be careful with change control and note that it is possible to look for contract extensions without additional bidding.

12.3.- Recognition of the need

A project can be triggered at the initiative of a user or by the technology area. In any case, users must be involved in defining needs and exploring possible solutions.

The recognition of the need corresponds to the analysis and design phases of the project in the Systems Development Lifecycle methodology (SDLC) described above. At this stage, exploring alternatives, analyzing the market, and testing different solutions is essential before committing to a final design.

In many cases, recognizing the need is only an initial diagnosis to justify allocating resources for the analysis and design of a solution. Either way, an estimate of the size of the problem (expected costs and benefits) is required to align the project against other projects competing for resources at this stage.

12.4.- Formalization of the contract

Once there is an understanding of the need, be it a custom development, a package, or a cloud application, the next step is to contact suppliers to measure their capabilities and receive their offers.

One way to initiate contact with a vendor is by issuing a Request for Proposal (RFP). This document can be as simple as a phone call or an email indicating the type of solution being sought. The RFP can be targeted to a specific company or open to the entire market. The supplier assigns a business leader who interviews the participants to prepare the requested proposal.

During this initial phase, the buyer can refine the requirements and better understand the supplier's capabilities. It is possible to work on the same project with more than one supplier as long as everyone understands that they are working with several companies and that there is only a final decision or commitment from either party once a contract is signed. It is also common to request a non-disclosure agreement (NDA) to protect privileged information shared at this stage.

The actual purchase is usually carried out by an area specialized in negotiation and acquisitions, generally known as the purchasing department. Depending on the amount, the purchasing department can acquire the defined solution with the recommended supplier or ask for more quotes from different vendors. They usually seek to demonstrate that the selected supplier is the most convenient for the company.

Governments and public entities have a set of laws governing the procurement process. In the United States, most federal government procurement is governed by the Federal Acquisition Regulations. In Canada, contracts are governed by the Government Contracts Regulations, which aim to ensure that government agencies in Canada "get the best value for Canadians while improving access, competition, and equity" [Government of Canada, 2023].

In Mexico, government purchases are the subject of the country's Political Constitution, which in its article 134 states:

> "The acquisitions, leases, and disposals of all types of goods, provision of services of any nature, and the contracting of works carried out shall be awarded or carried out through public bidding. Solvent proposals may be freely presented in a sealed envelope, which shall be opened publicly, to assure the State of the best available conditions in terms of price, quality, financing, timeliness, and other relevant circumstances."
>
> H. Congreso de la Unión, "Constitución Política de los Estados Unidos Mexicanos", Art. 134

Article 134 is operationalized, at the federal level, in the Law on Acquisitions, Leases, and Services of the Public Sector [Cámara de Diputados del H. Congreso de la Unión, 2014]. Different agencies in different states and countries have individual laws, but the processes are similar in scope and purpose. Figure 9.1 shows the general steps for bidding on a government contract.

Figure 1 2.1 - Steps for a government purchase process by public bidding

Minicase: who provides a better service?

For most people, taking a car to a mechanic is stressful. There are some excellent shops, but there are also some horror stories. The following are two similar stories with very different endings:

User one takes the car with a mechanic on Wednesday. The workshop asks the user to leave the vehicle for inspection and call in the afternoon to receive a quote. That afternoon the workshop has no information but tells the user that they will have a quote the following morning. The client gets the work proposal on Thursday at noon, approves it, and the shop promises that the car will be ready on Saturday morning, but they do not deliver. The car is finally out by Tuesday.

In case two, the user takes the car to the mechanic on Wednesday. The workshop asks the user to leave the vehicle for inspection and promises a quote by the afternoon of the following day. At noon on Thursday, the customer receives the work proposal that indicates that the shop has to order some missing parts, which will arrive on Monday, be installed on Tuesday, and that the car should be ready the following Wednesday. On Tuesday, the user gets a message that the vehicle is ready for pickup (one day earlier than promised).

Both workshops took the same time. Who gave a better service?

12.5.- Execution of the contract

Once a supplier is selected and a contract signed, control of the project returns to the development area handling the project. It is essential to understand the scope of the agreement. The supplier commits to specific delivery dates, and the customer commits to provide certain facilities and equipment to expedite the work.

The customer is responsible for ensuring that the received product complies with the requested specifications and is complete with the manuals and training agreed to in the contract.

The purchasing area must receive periodic progress reports to process any partial payment agreed upon in the contract.

During the execution of a contract, it is possible to find new areas of opportunity or require changes to the original design. It is essential to evaluate these modifications as they can affect the cost or delivery time of the final project. The way to handle changes is with a change control procedure where:

1. The area that identifies the opportunity fills out a form describing the change requested.
2. The project manager evaluates the appropriateness of forwarding the request to the supplier.
3. The supplier analyzes the modification request and decides if it can be examined or rejected.
4. The supplier examines the requested change and identifies its effect on price and delivery dates
5. The supplier writes a change proposal (with costs and times) and delivers it to the project manager
6. The project manager and the purchasing area analyze the change proposal and approve or reject it.

2.6.- Delivery of the project

A project is only complete once it is available to the user, and it does not require anyone from the vendor or the technology area to modify the software or tell the user what to do. There are two parts to declaring a project complete: It must run with no errors, and the user has to know how to operate it.

Eliminating errors requires testing. All the solution components must work well independently, but they must also work well together.

User training and data migration are also critical steps before releasing a project. The best software project is complete only if the user knows how to operate it.

Once the supplier has complied with everything stipulated in the contract, the project manager writes and signs a letter of acceptance. A copy of the letter goes to the purchasing department so they can process the final payments and close the contracts. At this time, the warranty period begins to run, and the company can sign a maintenance contract to ensure the continuous operation of the purchased application.

Minicase – We can buy any brand of equipment as long as it is the same as this supplier's 6394 model

Suppose a potential customer sends an RFP requesting pricing information for equipment of any brand. However, the description of the capabilities required copied the specifications of a competitor's computer. In that case, your competitor will likely have the advantage when it comes to offering products at better prices.

For example, an official RFP from a government office requested bids for computer equipment of any brand. The document specified that the equipment proposed had an Intel 6700 processor, four USB 3.0 ports, and a series of other specifications. The most interesting characteristic was that the equipment had to measure 50.8x30.5x5.08 centimeters and weigh exactly 2.7 kilograms.

If your company had worked with that potential customer before they released their RFP, the specifications might have been more general or the same as your product.

12.7.- Customer-supplier relationship in the pre-sales process

As discussed above, the purchasing process does not begin when a supplier is contacted or a request for proposal (RFP) is published. The process starts with the definition of the user's needs.

A supplier that learns of a project when an RFP is published (at the contract formalization stage) is probably too late to prepare a competitive bid. The requirements specifications could be for a technology from a different manufacturer, or it would not be easy to find a competitive advantage with the current specifications.

Technology providers must seek to engage with their customers from the stage of recognizing the need. This action will increase the chances that the solution the company plans to acquire fits the product the company is best prepared to supply. However, the customer-supplier relationship must not violate any law, create conflicts of interest, or involve acts of corruption.

In most cases, recognition of need begins with technology monitoring. In many companies, there is no specific area in charge of this function, or it belongs to a department usually short on resources and budget.

A company can benefit from supplier visits and available documentation to support the technology monitoring efforts. A provider may support the identification of opportunities with one or more of the following activities:

- Publication of information leaflets describing the technology
- Publication of case studies
- Organization of discussion groups
- Organization of conferences
- Visits to the technology areas of companies
- Relationship with user areas
- Publication of industry benchmarks
- Customer support in the preparation of bidding rules

12.8.- Roles that technology partners can take

A technology service provider (whether hardware, software, applications, consulting, or solutions) can play different roles in its clients' IT projects. Sometimes the work can be in an advisory scheme for a fee; at other times, the work must be done without compensation, seeking either to strengthen a relationship of trust or a long-term benefit to sell a solution later.

The leading roles that a technology partner can occupy are:

- As an advisor
- As a technical supervisor of a project
- As a solution integrator
- As a developer or builder of a project or module

The detail of each role is described below.

As an advisor (paid or unpaid)

A company can become an advisor to an organization and provide recommendations, seek information, design solutions, or even train end users. The supplier can charge a fee (fixed price or on time and materials) or work at no cost to the client. The consulting company will not be able to get involved in the implementation of the projects it is advising or charge a "finder's fee" to the winning suppliers of said contracts. If the service is pro bono, the company can get involved in the implementation, competing with other providers in the procurement process. In that case, the consulting supplier would be expected to have an advantage because it knows the project better and would be better suited to the solutions it typically markets.

As a technical supervisor of a project (with payment)

A project's technical supervision involves supporting the organization in the recognition, formalization, and administration stages of a contract. In this role, the supplier company must represent the interests of the client organization. It would typically be a remunerated activity (either at a fixed price or on time and materials), and the technical supervisor would be prohibited from participating in the execution of the project to avoid a possible conflict of interest.

As a solution integrator (with payment)

The role of solution integrator is a well-defined function in information systems development practice. The complexity of the technologies and the variety of specialists required add to the relevance of the integrator's role. It is particularly relevant in organizations that need more specialized human resources with sufficient experience to guarantee the project's success. In some cases, the integrator subcontracts the services of the rest of the providers; in others, his function is to coordinate different companies.

The work of an integrator is remunerated, usually at a fixed price. The integrator assumes the risks of implementation problems and project malfunctions.

As a developer or builder of a project or module

Another well-recognized role in the industry is that of developer or builder of a project. This role is the same as solution integrator from the perspective charged for delivering a complete solution. Generally, company contracts are fixed-price contracts defined from the beginning of the project.

12.9.- Summary

- The three phases of the procurement process are recognition of need, formalization of the contract, and contract administration.
- Recognition of the need starts with identifying and defining the company's requirements. The end product in this phase is a detailed RFP that would attract possible suppliers at reasonable prices.
- The second phase, the contract's formalization, is generally a very rigid process handled by areas specialized in negotiation or acquisitions. Depending on the investment required and the company's policies, the purchase can be awarded directly to a specific supplier, require two or more quotes from different suppliers, or even need a public bidding process.
- During the execution of the contract, the project is developed.
- It is essential to formally evaluate the modifications to the project that may arise after the signing of the contract, as they may affect the cost or delivery time of the final project.
- The customer is responsible for ensuring that the received product complies with the requested specifications and is complete with the manuals and training agreed to in the contract.
- Understanding the role that technology partners can play is crucial because it allows organizations to leverage external resources to find better solutions while avoiding violations of laws or conflicts of interest.
- For a supplier, it is vital to recognize the type of engagement they can have with a customer and plan their processes of pre-sales and sale of products and services.

12.10.- Review exercises

Questions

1. What are the three phases of the procurement process?
2. At what stage of the system lifecycle does need recognition occur?
3. Why is a specialized area needed in some organizations to formalize the contract?
4. What kind of follow-up should be given to the supplier during the execution of the contract?
5. What is change management, and why is it important?
6. At what stage of the technology acquisition process is it in a vendor's interest to engage with a potential customer?
7. What roles can a technology partner play with a customer during their acquisition process?

Exercises

1. Find a technology contract on the Internet and identify the following:
    a. What is the object of the contract?
    b. Who are the parties?
    c. What are the clauses?
2. Look for the RFP of a public bidding process
    a. What is being acquired?
    b. What are the events of the process and their dates?
    c. What are the requirements of the supplier?
3. Name five potential technology partners for a company.
4. Identify some activities (conferences, demonstrations, cases, etc.) available from technology providers.

Part V

Survival Skills

Chapter 13

Legal and Ethical Issues

"If thou be a leader, as one directing the conduct of the multitude, endeavour always to be gracious, that thine own conduct be without defect."

The Instructions of Ptah-Hotep, Egypt, 2375-2350 BC. C. [Gunn, 1906]

13.1.- Learning objectives

- Assess the cost to a manager of overlooking legal or ethical issues.
- Identify the elements of a contract.
- Know what a patent is and what kind of protection it grants.
- Know what copyright is and the rights it confers.
- Define the characteristics of an industrial secret.
- Know why technology represents new situations and challenges for applying ethical principles.
- Understand how to analyze and apply ethical principles.

13.2.- The cost to a manager of ignoring legal or ethical issues

When thinking about the work of a Chief Information Officer (CIO), the topic that comes to mind is computer equipment. The discussion could include software, data, and even telecommunications if you have some knowledge of the subject. But when you've worked in the area for a while, it's easy to see that a CIO's job, like any company executive, should also include legal and ethical issues.

Not so long ago, we read in the news that Travis Kalanick, the CEO of UBER, was resigning from his position in the company he helped create amid allegations of unethical behavior [Klainman, 2017]. Soon after, Harvey Weinstein, a powerful Hollywood producer, was fired from his own company and expelled from the Academy of Motion Picture Arts and Sciences for allegedly making inappropriate advances to actresses. The Hashtags #metoo and #timesup were born [BBC, 2022].

The phenomenon did not end there. Two years later, the fast food company McDonald's fired its CEO, Steve Easterbrook, for "showing poor judgment in engaging in a consensual relationship with an employee" [Weiner-Bronner, 2019].

Unfortunately, this is not something new either. In one of the oldest texts, the Instructions of Path-Hotep, written between 2375 and 2350 BC, one of the pieces of advice given to a future public servant is: "a thousand men have been ruined for the pleasure of a little time short as a dream" [Gunn, 1906].

Nor are these the only ethical problems that can cost careers. In 2016, the US Department of Justice accused 12 countries of receiving millionaire bribes from the Brazilian construction company Odebrecht in exchange for contracts [Matute Urdaneta, 2016]. As a result of the investigations, several presidents, ministers, and legislators from Central and South American countries are being investigated or have ended up in jail [Carranza, Robbins, and Dalby, 2019].

Today the New York Times publishes an entire section to address ethical violations in business (https://www.nytimes.com/topic/subject/ethics). How relevant are legal and ethical issues for a company?

Disregarding legal matters, not following the procurement processes in government sales, not reviewing in detail all the clauses of a contract, or not respecting copyright can lead to trials, millionaire losses, and even arrest warrants for some of the organization's executives. In 1998, a problem with an IBM project with Mexico City's Attorney General's Office led the company to pay a 37.5 million dollars settlement after a trial and arrest warrants issued to three senior executives of IBM and 19 former officials of the agency [Ortiz Moreno, 1998; DiarioTI, 1998].

13.3.- Contracts

Laws regulate the relationships and agreements between persons (physical or moral). Laws regulate marriages, the use and possession of property, and contracts, among others. A contract is an agreement between two or more parties to produce or transfer obligations or rights [Cámara de Diputados del H. Congreso de la Unión, 2021]. A contract offers and accepts a mutual commitment between several parties legally competent to agree.

The legal elements, components, interpretations, and scope of a contract are civil law matters not covered in this section. The objective here is to present only a general discussion of the elements and importance of a contract.

Minicase: I was missing a line in the contract

The Modern Systems Company (a fictitious name) signed a large contract with a government office to build a system that simplifies property tax payment management. Given that the Modern Systems Company is a solutions integrator, it hired Micro Developments, Inc. (another fictitious name) to manufacture the core software of the solution, signing a contract with them.

The project was completed on time and delivered to the client. The problem arose when the customer informed the Modern Systems Company that they wanted the source codes of the solution they bought because they wanted to share it with similar offices in other states with the same problem. Giving the client full ownership of a software system is not common practice, but the contract said that the government became the owner of the software produced and could give it away to others at will.

The Modern Systems Company called Micro Developments, Inc. to request the codes. The company refused to turn them over, arguing that they would no longer be able to sell their program in other states if they did that. Additionally, the assignment of the codes was outside the scope contract signed by the two companies.

The Modern Systems Company could not deliver the codes to the customer, so it did not fulfill its part of the contract. After several discussions, the company had to provide a working solution for the client and still return most of the customer's payment.

The moral of the story: It is essential to read contracts very well before signing them.

The idea behind a contract is that once an agreement is formalized, neither party can retract or do anything not permitted in the contract. A violation of the terms of a contract can land the offending party in court. If the contract is clear, the court can force the offending party to comply with the agreement. Therefore, if there is a contract, one can expect it to be fulfilled. Otherwise, the offender can be forced to yield at a higher cost.

The ultimate goal of a contract is that it never has to be used and that the parties comply with the stipulations. Confidence in the other party's compliance saves resources for all participants.

A contract can be written or verbal; however, a written agreement shows irrefutable proof of its existence.

In a contract, there are two main elements:

- Consent
- And an object that may be the subject of a contract

In our culture (and in most countries), consent is demonstrated by signing the contract. Most of the time, the signature is handwritten on paper where the contract clauses are. Sometimes it is required to sign or initial every contract page to ensure that the signed agreement is not changed.

Signing a contract means that you agree with everything the document says as it is. If there is an error or you want to avoid accepting a clause, it is better to sign only when the disputed clause is corrected or removed.

The object of the contract may be a good or service. There are different types of arrangements, for example:

- Buy-sell: the seller offers a good, and the buyer agrees to pay for it.
- Lease: The lessor allows the use of a property by the lessee, who pays rent for that use.
- Employment (provision of services): An employer offers an employee the opportunity to perform a job in exchange for payment.
- Other examples: Exchange, Donation, Loan, Deposit, etc.

Usually, a contract has three main sections: identification of the parties, clauses, and signatures. The first part introduces the participants, identifies who is signing the contract, and shows that they are legitimate company representatives or can legally represent themselves.

The second part includes the elements of the contract: objective, duration, the commitments of each party, and what happens if one of the parties does not comply, among others.

The third part includes the signatures of the participants (usually handwritten). It may also have the signatures of witnesses, who certify that the contract was signed without duress by qualified and authorized persons to do so. Some contracts also require a guarantor's signature to assume the contract's responsibilities in case one party fails.

13.4.- Patents

The idea of patent protection is that an inventor who has dedicated part of their life to creating a new device, developing a new process, or an innovative product can profit from their invention.

A patent is an exclusive right granted over an invention, which is a product or a process that provides, in general, a new way of doing something or offers a new technical solution to a problem. To obtain a patent, the inventor must disclose technical information about the invention in a patent application [WIPO, 2023].

A patent grants rights to the inventor generally for 20 years from the date of application. The patent is granted by a country and is valid only in its territory [USPTO, 2023]. The applicant must file a patent in all countries where he plans to take advantage of his invention.

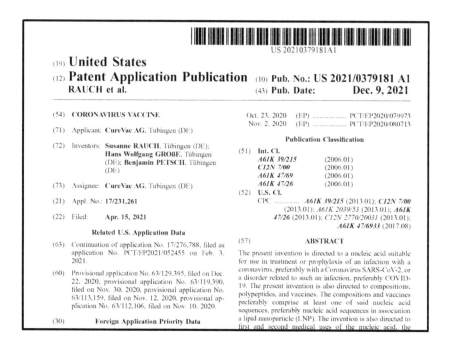

Figure 13.1 – US patent application for Coronavirus vaccine. Source: USPTO [2021]

A patent protects inventions, mechanisms, products, processes or solutions, etc., that meet three criteria [IMPI, 2013]:

1. **Novelty:** It is considered new, everything that is not state-of-the-art, that is, in the set of technical knowledge that has been made public through an oral or written description, by exploitation, or by any other means of dissemination or information, in the country or abroad.
2. **Inventive Step:** It is the creative process whose results are not deduced from the state-of-the-art in an obvious way for a technician in the field.
3. **Industrial Application:** It can be produced or used in any branch of economic activity.

One place to consult patent documents is on the website of the United States Patent Office (www.USPTO.gov). Another site where you can consult patent documents is Google Patents (https://www.google.com/?tbm=pts).

Minicase: Who is the parent of Windows?

Before Apple created its Lisa and Macintosh operating systems, the standard interface on a PC was "C:>_" or simply ">_."

Apple's operating system revolutionized user interfaces. Soon after, Microsoft releases Windows.

Apple considered Windows very similar to its operating system and sued Microsoft for copying its "look and feel."

In the middle of the fight between Apple and Microsoft, Xerox sues Apple arguing that its user interface copies the graphical user interfaces they developed in the 1970s at their Palo Alto Research Center (which Apple visited several times before designing its operating system).

The court dropped Xerox's lawsuit against Apple. An agreement between the parties likely caused the dropping of Apple's lawsuit against Microsoft.

Source: [Andrews 1993, Markoff, 1989]

Making the patent's content public shows the protected product and inspires technological improvements or new products to other inventors.

During the patent's life, the inventor may license it or sell it to whomever he sees fit. At the expiration of the 20 years of protection, anyone can use the patent without restriction. Some patents cease to be valuable before the end of their validity term, for example, when someone invents a superior product that renders the original obsolete. Other patents remain valuable even years after the end of their period. For example, medicines that at the end of the 20 years can be produced as generic medicines at low cost because the producer did not require an expense in research nor do they have to pay royalties.

13.5.- Copyright

A patent protects equipment, mechanisms, and apparatus. Software, diagrams, graphic designs, videos, and music (among others) are protected by copyright.

Copyright is composed of two parts [INDAUTOR, 2023]:

- **Moral rights** are the right to be recognized as the author and to be able to modify the work. Authors must be recognized as the author of their work even long after their death. This right never expires.

- **Economic rights** are the right of the author or third parties, determined by the author, to exploit the work commercially. This right is valid for the entire life of the author plus 50 years (in some countries for 75 or 100 years).

Copyright protection covers only expressions but not ideas, procedures, methods of operation, or mathematical concepts. In most countries, and under the Berne Convention, copyright protection is obtained automatically without registration or other formalities. The custom is to place the symbol © followed by the year of creation and the name of the rights owner. However, most countries have a registration and deposit system [WIPO, 2023b]. Registration can help resolve legal disputes that may arise. In Mexico, copyrights are registered at the Instituto Nacional del Derecho de Autor (National Institute of Author Rights) (INDAUTOR).

Figure 13.2 – Example of a copyright certificate issued by INDAUTOR.
Source: e-tam.com.mx [2015]

13.6.- Industrial secrets

On May 8, 1886, Dr. John Stith Pemberton sold the first glass of Coke at Jacobs' Pharmacy in downtown Atlanta [Coca-Cola, 2021]. The drink was patented in 1893. However, the formula has changed, and the new recipe is yet to be patented. If patented, the recipe would be known to all and could have been used and marketed by anyone since 1906.

An industrial secret is an invention or information that has an economic value and is unknown to the public.

The advantage that an industrial secret offers over a patent is that it does not expire, does not cost, and can be applied immediately. However, the downside is that you can't prohibit others from using the secret (if they know or discover it), and you lack solid legal protection against others using the secret in their patents.

Some famous trade secrets include:

- The recipe for Coca-Cola
- Google's search algorithm
- The secret recipe of Kentucky Fried Chicken
- Listerine
- WD-40
- The recipe for Krispy Kreme doughnuts

The idea of a secret is that it is not shared with the public. An industrial secret should never be part of a copyrighted document (by definition, a public record). Similarly, it is inappropriate to declare confidential a paper claiming copyright or accusing someone of espionage for downloading copies of patents filed by a company.

13.7.- Principles of ethics

When someone buys anything from an online store, they generally have to check a box accepting the site's terms and conditions before completing the purchase. Very few people read those terms, and most likely, one of them says that the company can share its customer's data with other companies and even publish the list of items a customer has purchased. Many clauses are there to legally protect the company in case of contingencies such as cyber-attacks or information leaks, but they are generally not expected to execute those clauses.

Even if a parson has nothing to hide, if a store made their shopping list public, surely that person would stop buying from that company. If the company published someone else's list, many customers would stop doing business with the store because, if they publish another client's list, what prevents them from doing the same to me? Such activity would not be illegal, but from the customer's point of view, it would violate their right to privacy, and they might consider it unethical.

The most challenging aspect for ethical thinkers today is that technological trends create new situations and questions humanity has not faced before. Some activities can be legal but considered unethical and, eventually, damage the company.

Society is just beginning to address the ethical issues and dilemmas posed by these technological advances. How can you know what is correct and convenient and what is not? How do you know in which cases an activity is legal but unethical?

Even understanding what is legal might be challenging. Old laws do not cover new behaviors. The government is beginning to pass laws against cybercrime (identity theft, for example), harassment, or intimidation (bullying), but it's hard to stay ahead of cybercriminals.

Ethics in an information society makes each person responsible for their actions. Everyone is accountable for everything they do, no matter how anonymous the act may seem. Individuals are responsible for the consequences their actions may inflict on others and society as a whole. Ethics refers to the principles of good and evil that individuals, acting with free will, use to guide their behaviors.

One way to think systematically about ethical principles is to follow in the footsteps of ethical analysis. A five-step process is [Laudon, 2019]:
1. Identify the facts
2. Define the conflict and the values involved
3. Identify participants
4. Identify the available courses of action
5. Identify the potential consequences of such actions

The decision maker may apply one or more ethical standards to choose a course of action. Some moral principles or rules valid in different cultures that have survived the passage of time are [Laudon, 2019]:

- **Golden Rule:** Do unto others as you would have them do unto you.
- **Immanuel Kant's categorical imperative**: if something is not suitable for everyone, it should not be done to anyone.
- **Descartes' rule of change:** If something cannot be done repeatedly, it should not be done at all.
- **Principle of utilitarianism:** Select the alternative that represents the greatest value
- **Risk aversion principle:** Take the alternative that involves less harm or lower cost
- **"No free lunch" rule:** Everything costs and everything is owned by someone else unless there is a specific statement about it

Working with ethics is an investment in the future. Most companies seek profits for a long time. Sacrificing the future for short-term gain can be too expensive for an organization.

One place to investigate behaviors considered appropriate in different professions is in the codes of ethics of professional associations. Some examples are:

- AIS Code of Ethics and Professional Conduct, Association for Information Systems, https://aisnet.org/page/MemberCodeOfConduct [AIS, 2022]
- ACM Code of Ethics and Professional Conduct, Association for Computing Machinery, https://www.acm.org/code-of-ethics [ACM, 2023]
- IEEE Code of Ethics, Institute of Electrical and Electronics Engineers, https://www.ieee.org/about/at-a-glance.html [IEEE, 2023]
- Code of Professional Ethics, Mexican Institute of Public Accountants, http://imcp.org.mx/wp-content/uploads/2015/12/Codigo_de_Etica_Profesional_10a_ed1.pdf [IMCP, 2015]

13.8.- Summary

- A contract is an agreement between two or more parties to produce or transfer obligations or rights. The document offers and accepts a mutual commitment between several parties legally competent to agree.
- A patent is an exclusive right granted over an invention, which is a product or a process that provides, in general, a new way of doing something or offers a new technical solution to a problem. The inventor must disclose technical information about the invention in a patent application to obtain a patent.
- Software, diagrams, graphic designs, videos, and music (among others) are protected by copyright.
- Copyright is composed of two parts [INDAUTOR, 2023]:
    - Moral rights are the right to be recognized as the author and to be able to modify the work.
    - Economic rights are the right of the author or third parties, determined by the author, to exploit the work commercially.
- An industrial secret is an invention or information that has an economic value and is unknown to the public.
- Ethics refers to the principles of good and evil that individuals, acting with free will, use to guide their behaviors. There are perfectly legal activities that can be considered unethical in some instances and, eventually, damage the company.

13.9.- Review exercises

Questions

1. What is a contract?
2. What can be the subject of a contract?
3. Mention a few different types of contracts
4. What are the pairs of a contract?
5. What does a patent protect, and how?
6. What is a copyright?
7. What rights does an author get with a copyright?
8. What is a trade secret?
9. What is ethics?
10. How are ethical dilemmas resolved?

Exercises

1. Find a contract on the Internet, and identify the object of the agreement, the clauses, and the participants.
2. Locate a patent, report its application date, what it claims, and the owner.
3. Find a copyrighted document. Who owns it?
4. List a trade secret not listed in this book.

Chapter 14

Negotiation and Sales

"Sell me this pen"

Jordan Belfort, played by Leonardo DiCaprio in "The Wolf of Wall Street," 2013.

14.1.- Learning objectives

- Define negotiation and understand what is negotiable.
- Identify the objectives of a negotiation.
- Identify the different negotiation strategies and know when to apply them.
- Understand the negotiation process.
- Understand the sales process.
- Master the concept of solution selling.

14.2.- Everything is a negotiation, but not everything is negotiable

When one thinks of negotiation and sales, it is common to concentrate on acquisitions of goods and services involving large amounts of money. Those activities are negotiation, but so is managing human resources in an office or deciding which movie to watch with a friend. A baby who can get her parents to get up at three in the morning to feed her, as unusual as it may seem, is negotiating. Everything is a negotiation.

Not everything is negotiable. Freedom, health, and honor are priceless. Culture and customs define certain limits to what can be negotiated. Ethical principles are fundamental in setting limits on negotiations.

Any human interaction is a negotiation and is something we unconsciously do from birth. However, people should pay more attention to the process.

Understanding the negotiation process can put us in a position where we have an advantage and can find opportunities to get what we seek.

Understanding what each participant is looking for and what they are willing to give up is essential. The same goes for knowing when to press and compromise in a negotiation.

14.3.- Objectives of a negotiation

Knowing your objectives (what you are looking for) is essential when entering a negotiation. Otherwise, how would you know if it is worth negotiating or if the goal has already been achieved?

An exercise designed by Prof. Mary Rowe [Rowe, 2001] illustrates interactions in a negotiation. The activity consists of simulating a negotiation. A group is divided into subgroups of two people, and each pair receives an imaginary two dollars to split between them. Each participant gets a card with instructions about their goals or the negotiation situation.

The game is repeated three times. The first time, each player receives a card with a target amount to be sought. Each player must agree with their counterpart to receive as much as possible from the two dollars but must try to reach the target amount. Amounts range from twenty-five cents to two dollars on each card.

Some couples have a simple process. If both participants are looking for twenty-five cents, everyone can achieve their goal and get more money than the amount requested. Other teams have a more complicated process, particularly when the sum of the two amounts exceeds two dollars. For example, if one player is looking for $1.25 and the other needs $1.50.

Among the concepts illustrated in this exercise are the resistance point (the amount a player is looking for) and the negotiating range (what remains between the reserve points) that can be positive or negative. [Lewiki, Barry, and Saunders, 2011]. This part of the exercise illustrates that one of the goals when negotiating can be the amount to gain.

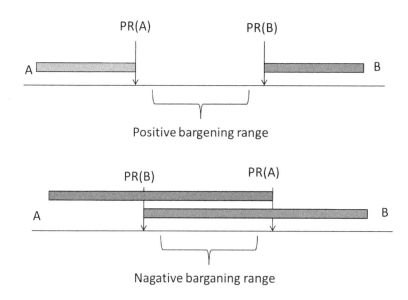

Figure 14.1.- Elements in a negotiation

In the second round, players change partners, and each player receives a new instruction card, replacing the initial one. The difference is that this time the card says to get as much as you can out of the two dollars but to consider (for example) that you have a reputation for being a great negotiator in your company and that you cannot let them down. The cards are different. They do not include a target amount. They talk about the player's reputation; the counterpart's past performance; or that one player is a public figure, and the negotiation could appear in tomorrow's paper.

This round illustrates two new elements of negotiation: the self (or reputation) and the process to follow.

Players return to their original partner in the third round and receive a new instruction card. This time, the cards talk about time limits and whether the other player can bring additional business in the future. Sometimes it is worth being more flexible in negotiation to obtain future gains. This phase illustrates the fourth objective: the relationship with the counterpart.

The four objectives of negotiation are the GRIP [Budjac, 2017]:
- (G) Gain
- (R) Relationship
- (I) I
- (P) Process

14.4.- Negotiation strategies

The exercise in the previous section is a zero-sum model. That is, a participant can win, lose, or reach an intermediate point, but what one party gains, the other loses. In that case, there are three possible negotiation strategies: Accommodating (giving two dollars to the counterparty), Competing (looking for the counterparty to be at zero), or reaching a compromise (50%-50% or 75%-25%, etc.).

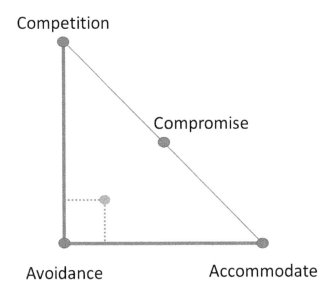

Figure 14.2.- Alternative negotiation strategies in a zero-sum model.
Source: [Rowe, 2002].

Why would someone choose to accommodate (yield) in a negotiation? The participant might be looking for an alternate benefit, like a long-term relationship or better conditions in a future negotiation. The accommodation option works well when the matter is unimportant, and it is more important to maintain the relationship. However, it is not advisable to always use it because you risk falling into depression or losing respect.

The alternative of competing is appropriate in case of emergency, or if you know you are right, and that is more important than maintaining the relationship. People do not expect to negotiate an order to abandon a sinking ship. It is advisable to use the competition strategy only when it is necessary.

There is an additional alternative in this case: the option of not negotiating. This option is advisable if the negotiation cannot produce a favorable result, the trading conditions are not adequate, or the result to be obtained is not worth the effort.

In real life, there are few zero-sum cases. Generally, negotiations have so many edges that it is always possible to find solutions other than all or nothing. It is possible to find something meaningful for each of the parties. This alternative is called collaboration, and it occurs when both parties make a profit. This course of action is known as the win-win model.

For example, if the deal is successful when selling a used car, both buyer and seller have gained something. The buyer bought a car at a reasonable price, and the seller made a fair profit in the process. Both participants can come out feeling like they won something.

The collaboration option (win-win) is almost always the most desirable alternative. It is essential to try to find a negotiated outcome that is beneficial to all participants.

If one of the five alternatives proposed is not followed, two undesirable options would be to seek revenge or go to the extreme of seeking revenge, even if that means a loss for both parties.

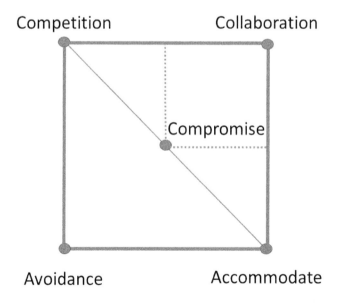

Figure 14.3.- It is preferable to look for the option of using the collaboration strategy (win-win). Source: [Rowe, 2002].

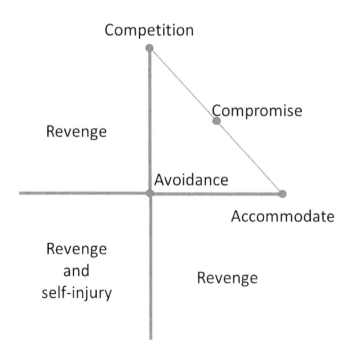

Figure 14.4.- Revenge, and revenge, even if both lose, are unwanted negotiation strategies. Source: [Rowe, 2002].

14.5.- The negotiation process

A negotiation can be divided into five steps. At each stage, some activities help improve the chances of a satisfactory outcome. This section only presents some of the more general recommendations for each phase. The steps are [Budjac, 2017]:

1. Preparation
2. Introduction
3. Initiation
4. Intensification
5. Closing

Preparation

The preparation stage occurs before the negotiation begins. In this stage, the negotiator gathers all the relevant information. It is essential to understand one's objectives and limitations, but also the counterpart's. This stage helps prepare a plan for the negotiation.

Define your objectives (gain, relationship, I, and process), and anticipate your counterpart's expectations. Know what points can be yielded and plan the arguments and counterarguments to use. Prepare an agenda and contingency plans in case of changes.

Introduction

The first seconds of the negotiation define the tone and style to follow. In this phase, the participants introduce themselves, exchange their data (name, title, and position), and try to establish their legitimacy and strength in the negotiation. Details such as body language, clothing, or the arrangement of chairs in the meeting can affect the process. Try to reduce the points that give advantages to the counterpart.

Initiation

When starting to negotiate, the first step consists in asking questions. Try to confirm the information gathered during the preparation phase and define which planned strategies will give the best results. Some moves at this stage are:
- Start with the more significant issues and deal with the small details later.
- Only make the first offer if you have no choice.
- Expect your first offer to be the best you can get.
- Ignore extreme positions (if someone starts asking for millions of dollars, ignore it and ask for a genuine offer).

Intensification

The negotiation details are refined to reach a final deal. Some effective tactics in this phase are:

- Reduce your position only if your counterpart does too.
- Keep the size of your changes in price relatively similar to your counterpart's. The size of the changes should get narrower as the negotiation progresses.
- Beware of proposing to split the difference, it can be taken as a new starting point, and you would have already lost half the way.
- You can distract by attacking irrelevant points of the proposal.
- You can bundle some difficult points with valuable points for your counterpart.

Closing

Until hands are shaken, or contacts signed, everything negotiated can be undone and canceled. Some techniques to facilitate this stage are:

- Create time pressure to force a shorter analysis.
- Offer small concessions, especially points not very relevant to you but valuable to the counterparty.
- It is not advisable to resort to ultimatums or threats to cancel everything unless you are willing to follow through on the threat.

14.6.- The sales process

Buying a product or service, especially for high-cost industrial solutions, usually requires a lengthy analysis. The process begins when the customer learns of the product's existence, analyzes it, sees if the purchase is convenient, initiates the negotiation, and acquires the product. Only some of the people who learn about the product buy it.

Many customers find out about the product's existence; some analyze it; few may decide to buy it, and perhaps one or two close the deal. From the seller's point of view, the process of taking a customer from when they do not know the product's existence to the point where the deal is closed is known as the sales pipeline. The idea is that the pipes have a wide entrance and a smaller exit.

The sales pipeline shows the customers' position in the process, defines the attention required by each customer, and can forecast sales by period [Horowitz, 2023]. Designing the pipeline requires dividing the process into stages. The number and duration of each step vary depending on the type of product to be sold. After a specific time at each step, a customer moves to the next stage or is off the list.

In the case of the sale of a computer system, the process can take six months, and the customer goes from being someone who saw the product at a conference, receives the visit of a sales representative, receives a proposal, negotiates a contract, and signs a contract. Many customers can see the product. Knowing how many of them will call and how many of those who call end up signing a contract, you can calculate the number of trade shows to attend and how often they are needed to complete the organization's sales goals.

This process works for items as varied as computer equipment, services, or college recruiting. In the case of the recruitment process for a university, potential students see the university's presentation, fill out a form indicating that they are interested, receive additional information and fill out the application, complete the admission exam, are admitted, and enroll. The pipeline, in this case, would have six stages and last approximately six months. If, for example, it is known that 20% of those who see a presentation fill out a form and 25% of those who fill out a form end up registering, it is possible to estimate that to complete a quota of 100 new students, it is necessary to make 20 presentations to groups of 100 potential students.

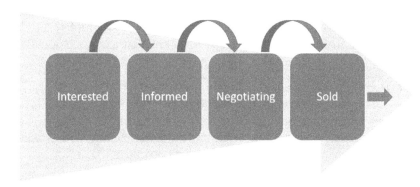

Figure 14.5.- Example of a sales pipeline. The customer goes from being interested, informed, negotiating the purchase, and completing the sale.

14.7.- Solution selling

One technique for bringing products closer to customers and securing a sale is to find the customer who needs the product and then make the sale. This process is called Solution Selling [Bosworth, 1994].

The sale of solutions is based on three premises:
1. No pain, no change
2. The only thing that motivates people to spend money is an unmet need.
3. In highly competitive markets, the advantage is in the sales process rather than in the product offered.

Managing pain

Pain is an unmet need. However, not all customers who have that need know they require the product. The unmet need is known as latent pain. The seller's job is to turn the latent pain into pain and then that pain into a vision (that fits the features, advantages, and benefits of the offered product). Thus, the pain cycle consists of three steps:

1. Latent pain
2. Pain
3. Vision

Minicase: Payment of salaries by bank deposit

For a sales representative for banking services, a company that pays its salaries using envelopes with cash is a customer with a latent pain. The seller's job is to turn that latent pain into pain and further turn it into a vision of the bank's services as a solution to the customer's needs.

Converting a latent pain to pain requires showing the costs of paying with cash and the savings of paying with direct deposit. The idea is to show the client they are losing money by paying the current way. The next step is to create a vision of the direct deposit system. The phrase to use is: "imagine how things would be if you could..."

If the customer visualizes the solution, what follows is to show that the bank's services best fit that vision. After that, the customer is the one that would request the product. The sale is automatic.

A salesperson trying to sell the idea of paying salaries by direct deposit to bank accounts should be looking for a customer who pays wages in cash (latent pain). The job is to help the client realize the costs and risks of paying with cash (pain). And work on creating a vision by stating: "imagine if you could pay all your employees at the same time without the disadvantages of paying cash."

Characteristics, advantages & Benefits

When managing pain, the vision being created must match the product being offered. It would make little sense to work to convince the customer to buy a competitor's product. Therefore, it is imperative to be clear about the product's characteristics, advantages, and benefits.

An example of this would be that bank A's automatic paycheck deposit system is easy to use, fast, and costs very little.

Participate in the buyer's vision

To guide the buyer in the transition from latent pain to vision, Michael Bosworth presents a nine-box vision process model [Bosworth, 1994]:

The process begins with the first column asking how things are currently done (identifying latent pain). Then it continues with the second column exploring various possible pains (expanding the pain). This phase is repeated for each additional latent pain. Finally, work is done on the third column, culminating in the confirmation of the vision. "From what I understood, if you could do (capabilities), you would fix your (pain)."

	Diagnose the reasons	Explore the impacts	Visualize capabilities
Open	Tell me about your (Pain); What is causing it?	In addition to you, who else faces that (Pain)? How?	What will be necessary to solve this (Pain) ?? May I suggest some ideas?
Control	That's because ...	This (Pain) is also causing ... If so, are there other areas that are also being affected?	And if there was a way to... would not it help? And if you could ...
Confirm	Then, the reasons for your (Pain) are (summary) ...	From what I understood then, that (Pain) ends up also affecting the areas ... so ...	From what I understood then, if you could (repeat abilities), would you solve your (Pain)?

Figure 14.6.- Nine-box vision process model [Bosworth, 1994]

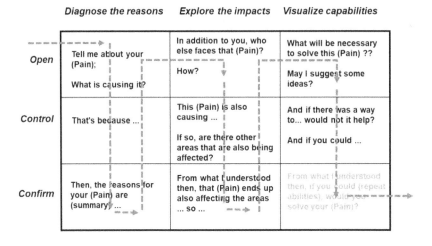

Figure 14.7.- Creating a vision [Bosworth, 1994]

Sometimes, the customer already has an idea of a vision, in which case the model of the nine boxes is handled a little differently in a process known as vision reengineering. The point here is to identify some differences between the proposed solution and the one the client has in mind and then work on those differences as the pains to be analyzed.

Vision reengineering begins in the two upper spaces of the third column to identify the current vision. The reengineering is completed by working columns one and two, considering the differences between the current solution and the desired one as pains. The exercise concludes in the last box of the third column.

Suppose the customer already has bank A's payroll deposit payment system in mind. Suppose that the main difference between banks A and B (which you represent) is that B has more branches. The job is to make that difference a significant pain. The final vision should include payment by direct deposit in a bank with more offices.

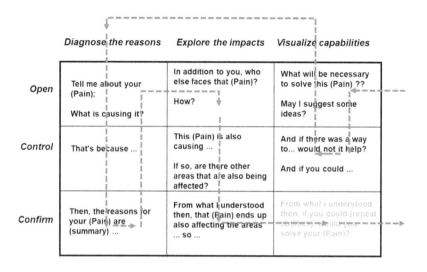

	Diagnose the reasons	Explore the impacts	Visualize capabilities
Open	Tell me about your (Pain); What is causing it?	In addition to you, who else faces that (Pain)? How?	What will be necessary to solve this (Pain) ?? May I suggest some ideas?
Control	That's because ...	This (Pain) is also causing ... If so, are there other areas that are also being affected?	And if there was a way to... would not it help? And if you could ...
Confirm	Then, the reasons for your (Pain) are (summary) ...	From what I understood then, that (Pain) ends up also affecting the areas ... so ...	From what I understood then, if you could (repeat capabilities) would you solve your (Pain)?

Figure 14.8.- Vision reengineering [Bosworth, 1994]

14.8.- Summary

- Any human interaction is a negotiation and is something we unconsciously do from birth, but things like health, freedom, or honor are not negotiable.
- The four elements of the objectives of a negotiation can be remembered by the acronym GRIP and are (G) Gain, (R) Relationship, (I) I, (P) Process.
- People can use different negotiation strategies: avoid, accommodate, compete, collaborate, and not negotiate. Most times, it is better to collaborate (win-win).
- The negotiation process consists of five steps: Preparation, Introduction, Initiation, Intensification, and Closing.
- One technique for bringing products closer to customers and securing a sale is to find the customer who needs the product, create a vision in the customer and then make the sale. This process is called Solution Selling.

14.9.- Review exercises

Questions

- What is a negotiation?
- Mention some non-negotiable elements
- How do you determine what is negotiable?
- How are the objectives of a negotiation defined?
- What trading strategies exist, and when should each be used?
- What are the steps of the negotiation process?
- What is the sales pipeline?
- What is solution selling?
- What is pain management?
- How can a vision be reengineered?

Exercises

1. Look for a video clip of a television program called "Pawn Stars" and analyze the negotiation steps that are followed in one of the negotiations of the program.
2. Look for an example of negotiation and determine the GRIP objectives of both parties.
3. Locate an example of solution selling.
4. Identify a product and a customer with a latent pain suitable for using the solution selling methodology.
5. Find the characteristics, advantages, and benefits of a CRM system.

Chapter 15

Presentation of Business Initiatives

"Hi, my name is Mark Lim, this is my beautiful wife Hanna, and we are the founders of Lollacup. We are here today seeking a one hundred thousand dollars investment for 15% equity stake in our company."

Mark Lim, Lollacup pitch, Shark Tank, 2012

15.1.- Learning objectives

- Differentiate between a business model and a business plan.
- Know the advantages of having a business plan.
- Know the content and format of a business plan.
- Identify the parts of a business plan.

15.2.- The importance of business plans

One of the reality-shows that emerged in the past years features entrepreneurs showing their projects to potential investors. The program is called Shark Tank, and there are versions of the show with investors from different geographies. Sharks ask tough questions of entrepreneurs about their proposals; after all, it's their money they'd be risking. Successful entrepreneurs secure a new partner and some funding for their projects.

In a private company, the situation is similar. Shareholders are risking their money on projects presented to them by different departments and areas of the organization. The technology area competes for approval against projects proposed by Marketing, Production, Finance, etc. Approval requires well-presented and clear proposals delivered in a language understandable by investors.

The language spoken in the shark tank is that of business proposals. It is about measuring the cost/benefit of the proposal and analyzing the risk it carries. The two ideas that shape the presentation are the business model and the business plan [Laudon and Traver, 2019].

- **A business model** is a group of activities designed to produce profit in a marketplace.

- **A business plan** is a document that describes the business model outlining goals and strategies.

Among the advantages of preparing a business plan is:

- It is a communication tool that can help secure funding
- It forces the designer to think about the elements of the business.
- If a business plan shows that the idea doesn't work, you can avoid a business failure before it starts.
- The document can serve as a guide during the implementation of the project.
- It can help recruit people necessary for the project's success.

15.3.- Elements of a business plan

Every business opportunity is different, and every situation is unique, yet certain elements are common to all business plans. Three factors are essential for investors [Nuno, Raskino, and Cox, 2021]:

- Project's value: Does the project generate new revenue? Does it increase sales or reduce costs? Does the project support the company's mission?
- Future costs and savings: What is being requested (money, resources, approval)? What are your financial indicators?
- Risks: What can fail (funding, regulation, infrastructure, reputation)? What is the probability that the project will not work as expected?

Another important point has to do with how the information is presented. In some literary novels, the reader is expected to read to the last chapter to understand specific critical details of the plot. In a business document, the reader expects answers to questions as quickly as possible. The business plan begins with a summary describing the project, needs, and risks.

A suggested organization for the document is as follows [Turban, Volonino, and Wood, 2015; Laudon, 2019]:

1. Cover letter
2. Executive summary
3. Business description
4. Market analysis
5. Competitive environment
6. Operation strategies
7. Financial analysis
8. Management team

15.4.- Cover letter

When a proposal is sent to a potential investor or partner, the document must be accompanied by a note explaining what would be received. The cover letter is an opportunity to show, on a single page, the project's objectives and needs.

The letter begins with the contact details and the greeting. The first paragraph is short and defines the purpose of the letter. You can start with: "Enclosed please find the proposal for..." or "following in our conversation, I am enclosing a copy of...".

The following two paragraphs describe the opportunity. It is vital to make clear what is being requested, what the business consists of, and why it is an excellent opportunity.

The closing paragraph thanks the readers for their attention and reiterates our availability to clarify doubts or provide additional information.

15.5.- Executive summary

The executive summary is placed at the beginning of the document, but it is the last part written. The section concentrates, on one page, all the elements of the project. Like the cover letter, it begins by clarifying what is requested, what the business consists of, and what the initiative's costs, benefits, and risks are.

This section has two objectives. The first one is to invite the reader to get more information about the project. The second one is to help the reader create a frame of reference to organize the ideas presented in the rest of the proposal.

One way to organize the executive summary is around the solution-selling process. Turn latent pain into pain, and create a vision matching the project's characteristics, advantages, and benefits.

On the shark tank show, the typical start of a presentation says, "I'm here to offer X% of my company in exchange for a $$ investment. The business consists of ... and promises a return on investment of %%" and then continues with the details of the project.

15.6.- Business description

The details of the business proposal formally start in this section. It describes the business opportunity. It answers the following questions: What is the opportunity? What is the value proposition? Why is it necessary? How is it going to be monetized? And What type of support is needed for the project?

The section starts by clarifying the objectives of the document. A business plan can have different types of purposes. Some examples are: securing financial support, getting approval, obtaining professional advice, reporting the project, or finding a partner or someone to add to the project.

The following section describes the project. It clarifies the type of business, how it works and the results expected.

The business description's third component explains why the project is essential. It describes the project's benefits for the client and why they will buy into the proposed solution. The value proposition describes the customer's need that is being solved and why they will come with us for that solution. Some value propositions are: reducing the purchase time, offering the lowest price, offering various products, or serving a niche market.

Part four describes how the project will be monetized. Every project costs money, and someone has to pay for the time of those involved, computer equipment, supplies, or programming. The project must leave sufficient benefits to recover costs and provide a reasonable profit. The monetization section explains how income will be obtained from the project.

Revenue from a project can come from the product or service being provided and can take the form of:

- **Advertising:** ads on the page (CNN, Disney, Facebook, Google)
- **Subscriptions:** Premium services (Spotify, Amazon Prime)
- **Transaction fee:** Commission for executing some service (Ticketmaster)
- **Sales revenue:** Profit from the sale of products (Walmart, Amazon, Dell)
- **Affiliation:** Seller commission for bringing you customers (Groupon)

If the benefits are tangible, the section explains how to measure them. If the project produces intangible benefits like improving a company's image or complying with a new law, the document must discuss its relevance.

Minicase: What is Amazon's business model?

Amazon.com, Inc. is today one of the most valuable companies in the world. It began operations in 1994 as an online bookstore. Today it is the largest retail sales company on the Internet.

Amazon not only derives its revenue from its sales, it also allows third parties to market its products on its website by charging a percentage of sales from them. Another way you make money is by allowing your affiliates to advertise on your platform.

Amazon also makes and sells some electronic devices like its Kindle tablets and has a service where it allows authors to print their books and sell them.

Amazon has several subscription services, such as Amazon Prime Video, known as Prime Video, which streams movies and shows (including exclusive programming). Kindle Unlimited, another subscription service, allows users to read unlimited e-books in exchange for a monthly payment.

Like many other businesses, Amazon does not have a pure revenue model but uses a mixed model.

15.7.- Market analysis

This section describes the target market for the project. Some products are designed for an extensive market, for example, Coca-Cola. In contrast, other products, like a bridal magazine, target a specific group.

A car is not accessible to everyone. A luxury model would not be accessible to everyone who can buy a car.

Markets can be segmented by purchasing power. Other ways to segment the market could be by geographic region, gender, profession, or age.

The section describes the target market. Describes its size and defining characteristics.

15.8.- Competitive environment

Once the product and market have been defined, the following section answers the question of who else is serving the same market. Not all competitors selling the same product compete with the project, as they may suit different needs. For example, even if Porsche and Ford sell cars, they sell to different types of customers.

On the other hand, companies in different lines could be looking for the money or time of our clients and represent a significant competition. For example, Starbucks is a competitor to McDonald's. People go to one or the other, but not to both places on the same day.

Another crucial point to address in this section is to define the competitive advantage that would be had over the identified competition.

15.9.- Operation strategies

Depending on the product or service provided, this section describes the business elements relevant to the proposal. For example:

- Place of operation
- Required equipment or facilities
- Logistics
- Quality control
- Customer Service
- Organizational structure

The number and type of elements to be discussed will depend on the document's target audience and the type of product or service to be developed.

15.10.- Financial analysis

This section discusses the project from the point of view of its costs and benefits. It is important to remember that money changes in value over time and that it is different to receive one hundred dollars today than in a year. Therefore, it is vital to present cash flows for the project's expected duration.

Some relevant indicators are the amount to be invested, the payback period, the net present value, and the internal rate of return.

A common practice is to present three scenarios in each proposal: the expected scenario, the optimistic scenario, and a pessimistic scenario (most likely, best case, and worst case). If all alternatives are favorable, the project might be approved. If the best case scenario is pessimistic, there is not much point in continuing with the project. However, mixed results will prompt a review of the level of risk and the probability that each scenario occurs to determine whether or not to proceed with the project.

Excel is a potent tool, and if a model is not producing the results needed for approval, it's tempting to change the income estimate to make the results acceptable. This practice is dangerous because if the initial assessment was honest and well calculated, obtaining the results promised in the modified analysis would be difficult.

It is convenient to modify the analysis when measuring the effort necessary to make a project profitable. For example, if seeing a project turns out that sales in year three must be at least $18,000 for the net present value (NPV) and internal rate of return (IRR) to be favorable, we must ask ourselves how difficult it is to reach $18,000 in sales. If the answer, in all honesty, is that this number is not a problem, then you can present the project to the authorities that analyze it and request the budget to carry it out. If, on the other hand, reaching $18,000 in sales requires an extraordinary effort that has never been done before, the project will likely never deliver the results necessary to be considered profitable.

It is much better to identify a potential problem when the project is in the planning and analysis stage than to wait for implementation to realize that the wrong decision has been made.

A good analysis can provide confidence that the project has potential and allow decision-makers to compare different investment alternatives. IRR and NPV will enable you to compare the expected results of diverse projects such as technology, marketing, or production, to name a few. These analyses allow you to make the best decision for the organization.

15.11.- Management team

One aspect sometimes overlooked in business plans is the team of people required to develop and operate on the project. If you already have a team, it is essential to list their skills and experiences to show the potential investor that the project has a greater chance of success.

If you need to recruit people, listing the skills and experiences required can help determine if the organization already has the resources, estimate the complexity of training current staff, or identify potential problems in locating new people to fill the roles and perform the necessary activities.

15.12.- Summary

- A business model is a group of activities designed to produce profit in a marketplace.
- A business plan is a document that describes the business model outlining goals and strategies.
- Among the advantages of preparing a business plan is:
  - It is a communication tool that can help secure funding
  - It forces the designer to think about the elements of the business.
  - If a business plan shows that the idea doesn't work, you can avoid a business failure before it starts.
  - The document can serve as a guide during the implementation of the project.
  - It can help recruit people necessary for the project's success.
- A suggested organization for a business plan includes:
  1. Cover letter
  2. Executive summary
  3. Business description
  4. Market analysis
  5. Competitive environment
  6. Operation strategies
  7. Financial analysis
  8. Management team

15.13.- Review exercises

Questions

1. What is a business model?
2. What is a business plan?
3. What are the advantages of having a business plan?
4. What parts does a business plan contain?
5. What is the value of the cover letter?
6. What is the objective of an executive summary?
7. Which competitors are worth analyzing in competitive analysis?
8. What indicators go into the financial analysis?

Exercises

1. For each of the five revenue models listed in the business description section, find an example of one Internet company using it.
2. Choose one of the companies from the previous exercise and define its type of business, target market, competitive environment, competitive advantage, operating strategies, and management team.
3. Find a clip from the reality show "Shark Tank" where an entrepreneur is pitching a product. Check which business plan elements listed in this chapter are used in the proposal.

References

Chapter 1

[Apple Insider, 2023] Apple Insider, "Apple Watch" ai, 2023, accessed January 2023 at https://appleinsider.com/inside/apple-watch

[Avast, 2023] Avast, "What is Internet Streaming and How Does it Work?" Avast, 2023, consulted January 2023 in https://www.avast.com/c-what-is-streaming?redirect=1

[Companiesmarketcap, 2023] companiesmarketcap, "Largest Companies by Market Cap" companiesmarketcap.com, consulted January 2023 at https://companiesmarketcap.com/

[Davis & Olson, 1985] Davis, G.B., and Olson, M.H., "Management Information Systems: Conceptual Foundations, Structure, and Development" ISBN: 978-0070158306, second edition, McGraw-Hill, 1985.

[Dolan & Peterson-Withorn, 2023] Dolan K., & Peterson-Withorn, C. (eds.), "Forbes World's Billionaires List: The Richest in 2022," Forbes, 2023, accessed January 2023 in https://www.forbes.com/billionaires/

[Kharpal, 2020] Kharpal, A., "Apple Watch outsold the entire Swiss watch industry in 2019," CNBC, February 2020. Retrieved January 2023 on https://www.cnbc.com/2020/02/06/apple-watch-outsold-the-entire-swiss-watch-industry-in-2019.html

[McFarlan, 1984], McFarlan, W., "Information technology changes the way you compete," Harvard Business Review., Vol. 62 Issue 3, p98-103. May/Jun 1984.

[Montredo, 2019] Montredo, "Top 10 Swiss Watch Brands" Montredo.com May 2019, consulted in January 2023 in https://www.montredo.com/top-10-swiss-watch-brands/

[Ohmae, 1991] Ohmae K., "The Mind of the Strategist: The Art of Japanese Business" ISBN: 978-0070479043, McGraw-Hill, New York, 1991.

[Porter, 1980] Porter, M. E. "Competitive Strategy" ISBN 978-0-684-84148-9. Free Press, 1980.

[Porter, 2005] Porter, M. "The CEO as Strategist" in "Strategy bites back: It is a lot more, and less, than you ever imagined" Henry Mintzberg, Bruce W. Ahlstrand, and Joseph Lampel (eds.) pp. 45, Pearson Education, 2005.

[Porter and Millard, 1985] Porter, M.E., & Millard, V.E., "How Information Gives You Competitive Advantage," Harvard Business Review, Vol. 63 Issue 4, pp. 149-160, July-August 1985.

[Selectra, 2023] Selectra, "Las mejores plataformas de streaming en México: Netflix, Disney +, Amazon Prime y más" Selectra, 2023, consulted January 2023 in https://selectra.mx/streaming

Chapter 2

[9001Academy, 2023] 9001Academy, "What is ISO 9001?", 9001 Academy, 2023, accessed January 2023 in https://advisera.com/9001academy/what-is-iso-9001/

[Anand, 2019] Anand, A.; "The Service Value Chain, and Service Value Streams" ITIL 4: Connecting key concepts – Part 4, AXELOS 2019, accessed January 2023, in https://www.axelos.com/resource-hub/blog/itil-4-connecting-key-concepts-part-4

[ASQ, 2023] ASQ, "What is the Plan-Do-Check-Act (PDCA) Cycle?", ASQ, 2023, accessed January 2023 in https://asq.org/quality-resources/pdca-cycle

[Barrows, 2019] Barrows, E., "What Is Strategy Execution?" American Management Association, January 24, 2019, consulted January 2023, in https://www.amanet.org/articles/what-is-strategy-execution/

[Hanna et al., 2009] Hanna A.; Windebank J.; Adams S.; Sowerby J.; Rance S.; Cartlidge A.; "ITIL V3 Foundation Handbook" ISBN: 9780113311989, The Stationary Office, Norwich, UK, 2009.

[Humphrey, 1988] Humphrey, W. S. "Characterizing the software process: a maturity framework" IEEE Software, 5 (2), March 1988.

[ISACA 2023] ISACA, "COBIT an ISACA Framework: Effective IT Governance at your Fingertips" ISACA 2023, consulted in January 2023 in https://www.isaca.org/resources/cobit

[ISO, 2023] International Standards Organization, "ISO 9000 Family: Quality Management" ISO, 2023, accessed January 20323 in https://www.iso.org/iso-9001-quality-management.html

[Kaplan and Norton, 1992] Kaplan R.; Norton D.; "The Balanced Scorecard – Measures That Drive Performance" Harvard Business Review, Vol. 70, Issue 1, January–February 1992.

[Kaplan and Norton, 2004] Kaplan, R.; and Norton, D.; "How strategy maps frame an organization's objectives" FINANCIAL EXECUTIVE, Vol. 20, Issue 2, March/April 2004.

[Lankhorst et al., 2009] Lankhorst, M., et al., "Enterprise Architecture at Work", The Enterprise Engineering Series, ISBN: 978-3-642-01309-6, Springer-Verlag Berlin Heidelberg, 2009.

[Nag, Hambrick, & Chen, 2007] Nag, R.; Hambrick, D.C.; Chen, M. "What is strategic management, really? Inductive derivation of a consensus definition of the field." Strategic Management Journal (John Wiley & Sons, Inc.), Vol. 28, Issue 9, September 2007.

[Neely, Adams, & Crowe, 2001] Neely, A.; Adams, C.; and Crowe, P.; "The performance prism in practice" Measuring Business Excellence, Vol. 5, Issue 2, 2001.

[Ohmae, 1991] Ohmae K., "The Mind of the Strategist: The Art of Japanese Business" ISBN: 978-0070479043, McGraw-Hill, New York, 1991.

[Porter, 1980] Porter, M. E. "Competitive Strategy" ISBN 978-0-684-84148-9. Free Press, 1980.

[Porter, 1996] Porter, M., "What Is Strategy?" Harvard Business Review, Vol. 74 Issue 6, Nov/Dec96.

[Powell, 2012] Powell, C.; "It Worked for Me: In Life and Leadership" ISBN: 978-0062135131, Harper, 2012.

[Roncancio, 2018] Gabriel Roncancio G.; "Qué es el Balanced Scorecard o Cuadro de Mando Integral? Un Resumen" Pensemos, November 2018, accessed January 2023 in https://gestion.pensemos.com/que-es-el-balanced-scorecard-o-cuadro-de-mando-integral-un-resumen

[Smart Business, 2017] Smart Business, "ISO 9001:2015 Quality Management System Main clauses" Smart Business, 2017, accessed January 2023 in https://smartbusinesseg.com/iso-90012015-quality-management-system-requirements/

[Weill & Ross, 2004] Peter Weill, Jeanne W. Ross, "IT governance: how top performers manage IT decision rights for superior results" ISBN:781591392538, Harvard Business Press, 2004.

[White, 2019] Sarah K. White, S. K.; "What is COBIT? A framework for alignment and governance" CIO, January 2019, consulted January 2023 in https://www.cio.com/article/3243684/what-is-cobit-a-framework-for-alignment-and-governance.html

Chapter 3

[Alighieri, 1305] Alighieri, D.; "De vulgari eloquentia" Cambridge Medieval Classics, Series Number 5, ISBN: 978-0929837444, Cambridge University Press, Cambridge, 2005.

[Kirchmer, 2017] Kirchmer, M, "High Performance through Business Process Management: Strategy Execution in a Digital World" Third Edition, ISBN: 978-3-319-51219-4, Springer, 2017.

[Lankhorst, et al., 2009] M. Lankhorst et al.; "Enterprise Architecture at Work" The Enterprise Engineering Series, ISBN: 978-3-642-01309-6, Springer-Verlag, Berlin Heidelberg, 2009.

[Minoli, 2008] Minoli, D.; "Enterprise architecture A to Z: frameworks, business process modeling" SOA, and infrastructure technology, ISBN 978-0-8493-8517-9, CRC Press, 2008.

[Nextech, 2021], Nextech Education Center, "¿Qué es BPMN y para qué sirve?" May 2021, accessed January 2023 in https://nextech.pe/que-es-bpmn-y-para-que-sirve/

[Object Management Group, 2023], Object Management Group, "About the Business Process Model and Notation Specification Version 2.0" 2023, accessed January 2023 in https://www.omg.org/spec/BPMN/2.0/

[Richardson, Chang & Smith, 2020] Richardson, V., Chang, C., Smith, R, "Accounting information systems" ISBN:978-1260571080, McGraw-Hill, 2020.

[Weske, 2012] Weske, M., "Business Process Management: Concepts, Languages, Architectures" Second Edition, ISBN: 978-3-642-28615-5, Springer, 2012.

[Wikipedia, 2023] Wikipedia "Internal combustion engine" accessed January 2023 in https://en.wikipedia.org/wiki/Internal_combustion_engine

Chapter 4

[Cadbury, et al, 1992] Cadbury, A., et al., "Report of the committee on the financial aspects of corporate governance" The Committee on the Financial Aspects of Corporate Governance and Gee and Co. Ltd., 1992, accessed January 2023 in https://ecgi.global/sites/default/files//codes/documents/cadbury.pdf

[Drucker, 2008] Drucker, P. F.; "Management: Revised Edition", ISBN: 978-0061252662, Harper-Collins Publishers, New York, 2008.

[Leavitt and Whisler, 1958] Leavitt, H.; and Whisler, T.; "Management in the 1980's." Harvard Business Review, Vol. 36, Issue 6, November-December, 1958.

[Selig, 2008] Selig, Gad J., "Implementing IT Governance: A Practical Guide to Global Best Practices in IT Management", ISBN: 978 90 8753119 5, Van Haren Publishing, 2008.

[Weill & Ross, 2004] Peter Weill, Jeanne W. Ross, "IT governance: how top performers manage IT decision rights for superior results", ISBN:781591392538, Harvard Business Press, 2004.

Chapter 5

[Alanís, 2020], Alanís, M., "La Transformación Digital del Gobierno: Misma Tecnología, Diferentes Reglas y Mucho Más en Juego" ISBN: 9798616079961, Amazon, Middleton, DE, 2020.

[Alanís, 2021] Alanís, M., "Administración de Poyectos de Inteligencia de Negocios" ISBN: 9798745505874, Amazon, Columbia, SC, 2021.

[Baca Urbina, 2015] Baca Urbina, G. "Ingeniería Económica" ISBN: 9786071512444, McGraw-Hill Interamericana, Mexico City, 2015.

[Cameron, 1963] Cameron, William Bruce, "Informal Sociology, a casual introduction to sociological thinking" Random House, New York. 1963.

[Cemex, 2021] Cemex, "Sarbanes Oxley Act" consulted January 2023 in https://www.cemex.com/investors/corporate-governance/sarbanes-oxley-act#navigate

Chapter 6

[Asimov, 1983] Asimov, I.; "The Roving Mind" ISBN: 0-87975-201-7, Prometheus Books, Buffalo N. Y., 1983.

[Devaraj and Kohli, 2000] Devaraj, S.; and Kohli, R.; "Information Technology Payoff in the Health-Care Industry: A Longitudinal Study" Journal of Management Information Systems, Vol. 16, No. 4; M.E.Sharpe, Inc.; 2000.

[Kohli and Sherer, 2002] Kohli, R.; Sherer, D.A.; "Measuring Payoff of Information Technology Investments: Research Issues and Guidelines" Communications of the Association for Information Systems; Vol. 9, Article 14; 2002, accessed January 2023 in https://aisel.aisnet.org/cais/vol9/iss1/14

[Kohli, Sherer, & Barton, 2003] Kohli, R.; Sherer, D.A.; Baron, A.; "IT Investment Payoff in E-Business Environments: Research Issues" Information Systems Frontiers 5:3, Kluwer Academic Publishers, The Netherlands, 2003.

[Naegle and Ganly, 2020] Naegle, R.; and Ganly, C.; "Tell an IT Value Story That Matters to Business Leadership" Gartner, ID G00385725, Published 30 April 2019 - Refreshed 13 October 2020.

[NetSD, 2019] NetSD, "¿Por qué las empresas mexicanas deben invertir en tecnología?" NetSD, 2019, consulted in January 2023 in https://netsd.mx/empresas-mexicanas-invertir-tecnologia/

Chapter 7

[Buffett, 2002] Warren Buffett, W.; "Chairman's Letter – 2001" Berkshire Hathaway (February 28, 2002). consulted January 2023 at https://www.berkshirehathaway.com/letters/2001pdf.pdf

[Edmead, 2020] Edmead, M.T., "Using COBIT 2019 to Plan and Execute an Organization's Transformation Strategy" ISACA Industry News, ISACA, September 28, 2020, consulted January 2023 at https://www.isaca.org/resources/news-and-trends/industry-news/2020/using-cobit-2019-to-plan-and-execute-an-organization-transformation-strategy#

[Harmer, 2013] Harmer, G., "Governance of Enterprise IT based on COBIT 5: A Management Guide" ISBN: 978-1-84928-519-3, IT Governance Publishing, Cambridgeshire, UK, 2013

[ISACA, 2018-1], ISACA, "COBIT® 2019 Framework: Governance and Management Objectives" ISBN 978-1-60420-764-4, ISACA, 2018.

[ISACA, 2018-2] ISACA "COBIT® 2019 Framework: Introduction and Methodology" ISBN: 978-1-60420-644-9 ISACA, USA, 2018.

[ISACA, 2023-1] ISACA, "COBIT CASE STUDIES" ISACA, 2023 consulted January 2023 at https://www.isaca.org/resources/cobit/cobit-case-studies

[ISACA 2023-2] ISACA, "COBIT Over the Years" ISACA, 2023, consulted January 2023 at https://www.isaca.org/why-isaca/about-us/isaca-50/cobit-over-the-years

[Lainhart, 2018] Lainhart, J., "Introducing COBIT 2019: The Motivation for the Update?" COBIT Focus, October 29, 2018, consulted January 2023 at https://www.isaca.org/resources/news-and-trends/industry-news/2018/introducing-cobit-2019-the-motivation-for-the-update

[Volders and Jong, 2016] Volders, G. and Jong, K. "Implementing COBIT 5 at ENTSO-E" Industry News, ISACA, 2016, consulted January 2023 at https://www.isaca.org/resources/news-and-trends/industry-news/2016/implementing-cobit-5-at-entso-e

[Vyas, Al Ghait, Al Yaqoobi, Hasan, 2016] Vyas, V; Al Ghait, J.; Al Yaqoobi, A.; and Hasan, S.J.; "Dubai Customs COBIT 5 Implementation" Industry News, ISACA, 2016, consulted January 2023 at https://www.isaca.org/resources/news-and-trends/industry-news/2016/dubai-customs-cobit-5-implementation

Chapter 8

[CIO Source, 2018] CIO Source, "The Ideal Structure for an IT Department in a Growing Business" CIO Source, June 29, 2018, accessed December 2021 in https://www.ciosrc.com/blog/the-ideal-structure-for-an-it-department-in-a-growing-business/

[Drucker, 2008] Drucker, P. F.; "Management: Revised EdiTIon," ISBN: 978-0061252662, Harper-Collins Publishers, New York, 2008.

[Essent, 2021] Essent, "The Top 10 Benefits of Outsourcing IT through Managed Services", ESSENT, 2021, accessed January 2023 in https://www.essent.com/News/Blog/The-Top-10-Benefits-of-Outsourcing-IT-through-Managed-Services-284-24.htm

[Executech, 2022] Executech, "Advantages and Disadvantages of IT Outsourcing," Executech, 2022, accessed January 2023 in https://www.executech.com/insights/advantages-and-disadvantages-of-it-outsourcing/

[Lozhka, 2021] Lozhka, M.; "IT Outsourcing Advantages and Disadvantages" LANARS, 2021, accessed December 2021 in https://lanars.com/blog/it-outsourcing-advantages-and-disadvantages

[MJV Team, 2020] MJV Team, "IT Outsourcing: what is it and what are the main benefits for your company?" MJV, 12/06/2020, retrieved December 2021 from https://www.mjvinnovation.com/blog/it-outsourcing-what-is-and-benefits/

[Scott, Hill, and Mingay, 2020] Scott, D.; Hill, J.; Mingay, S.; "Balancing Your Approach to IT Centralization, Decentralization and Federation" Gartner, ID G00728653, August 26, 2020.

[Weill & Ross, 2004] Weill, P.; and Ross, J. W.; "IT governance: how top performers manage IT decision rights for superior results," ISBN:781591392538, Harvard Business Press, 2004.

Chapter 9

[Brooks, 1972] Brooks, F.P. "The Mythical Man Month: Essays on Software Engineering"," Addison-Wesley Publishing Company, 1972.

[Chaudhari, 2016] Chaudhari, K.; "Importance of CMMI-DEV in COBITbased IT Governance" COBIT Focus; 4 January 2016, retrieved January 2023 from https://fdocuments.us/document/importance-of-cmmi-dev-in-cobit-based-it-governance.html

[Ford, 1922] Ford, H. in collaboration with Crowther, S., "My Life and Work" Doubleday, Page & Company, New York, 1922.

[Gefen and Zviran, 2006] Gefen, D.; Zviran, M.; "What can be Learned from CMMI Failures?" Communications of the Association for Information Systems, Vol. 17, 2006.

[Hammer, 1990] Hammer, Michael "Reengineering Work: Do not Automate, Obliterate" Harvard Business Review, Vol. 68, No. 4, 1990.

[Humphrey, 1988] Humphrey, W. S; "Characterizing the software process: a maturity framework" IEEE Software. 5 (2), March 1988.

[Kendall & Kendall, 2005] Kendall, K.E., and Kendall J.E. "Systems Analysis and Design" Sixth Edition, Pearson Education, 2005.

[Lankhorst et al., 2009] Lankhorst, M., et al.; "Enterprise Architecture at Work" The Enterprise Engineering Series, ISBN: 978-3-642-01309-6, Springer-Verlag Berlin Heidelberg 2009.

[Laudon and Laudon, 2020] Laudon, K.C. and Laudon, J.P. "Management Information Systems: Managing the Digital Firm" ISBN: 978-0135191798, Pearson, 2019.

Chapter 10

[Agutter, 2012] Agutter, C. "ITIL ® Foundation Essentials The exam facts you need" ISBN: 978-1-84928-400-4, IT Governance Publishing, Cambridgeshire, UK, 2012.

[Anand, 2019] Anand, A. "The Service Value Chain, and Service Value Streams" ITIL 4: Connecting key concepts – Part 4, Axelos, May 15, 2019, consulted January 2023 in https://www.axelos.com/resource-hub/blog/itil-4-connecting-key-concepts-part-4

[Axelos 2021] Axelos, "City of Pittsburgh: Using ITIL for better public service provision" Axelos, 2021, accessed January 2023 in https://www.axelos.com/resource-hub/case-study/pittsburgh-itil-better-public-service-provision

[Axelos, 2023] Axelos, "What is IT Service Management?" Axelos, 2021, retrieved January 2023 from https://www.axelos.com/certifications/itil-service-management/what-is-it-service-management

[Gartner, 2023] Gartner, "IT Services" Information Technology Glossary, Gartner, 2021 accessed January 2023 in https://www.gartner.com/en/information-technology/glossary/it-services

[Gutierrez, 2018] Gutierrez, H. "Grupo Bimbo: Winning the ITIL Experience Award ITIL - Case Study" Axelos, 2018, retrieved January 2023 from https://www.axelos.com/resource-hub/case-study/grupo-bimbo-winning-the-itil-experience-award

[Hertvik, 2019] Hertvik, J. "What is ITIL Service Delivery?" Service Management Blog, September 6, 2019, BMC, 2019, accessed December 2021 in https://www.bmc.com/blogs/itil-service-delivery/

[Källgården, 2019] Källgården, O. "Spotify: An ITIL® Case Study" Axelos, 2019, consulted January 2023 in https://www.axelos.com/resource-hub/case-study/spotify-itil-case-study

[Kempter, 2021] Kempter, S. "Checklist SLA OLA" ITIL Process Map, 2021, accessed December 2021 in https://wiki.en.it-processmaps.com/index.php/Checklist_SLA_OLA

[Lankhorst, et al., 2009] M. Lankhorst et al. "Enterprise Architecture at Work" The Enterprise Engineering Series; ISBN: 978-3-642-01309-6, Springer-Verlag Berlin Heidelberg 2009.

[Surden, 1976] Surden E. "Privacy laws may usher in 'Defensive DP'" Interview of Grace Murray Hopper, Computerworld, Volume 10, Number 4, January 26, 1976, Computerworld, Inc., Newton, Massachusetts, now published by IDG Enterprise, 1976.

Chapter 11

[Dickinson, 2018] Dickinson, D., "'Fake news' challenges audiences to tell fact from fiction" UN News, May 2018 Consulted January 2023 in https://news.un.org/en/audio/2018/05/1008682

[Friedman, 2005] Friedman, T.L., "It's a Flat World, After All," New York Times Magazine, April 3, 2005, pp. 32-37, New York, 2005.

[History, 2020] History.com Editors "Arab Spring" published January 2018, updated January 2020, consulted January 2023 in https://www.history.com/topics/middle-east/arab-spring

[Kahn & Dennis, 2022] Kahn, R., & Dennis M.A. "Internet Computer Network" Encyclopædia Britannica, Published June 2020, updated November 2022, consulted January 2023 in https://www.britannica.com/technology/Internet

[Laudon & Traver, 2018] Laudon, K. C., & Traver, C. G. "E-commerce: Business, Technology, Society" 14th Edition, ISBN: 9781292251707, Pearson, 2018.

[Poe, 1836] Poe, E.A., "Maelzel's Chess-Player" Southern Literary Messenger, April 1836.

[Porter, 2001] Porter M.E, "Strategy and the Internet" Harvard Business Review. March 2001, Vol. 79, Issue 3, pp. 62-78.

Chapter 12

[Alanis, 2020] Alanís, M. "La Transformación Digital del Gobierno: Misma Tecnología, Diferentes Reglas y Mucho Más en Juego" ISBN: 9798616079961, 2020.

[Cámara de Diputados del H. Congreso de la Unión, 2014] Cámara de Diputados del H. Congreso de la Unión "Ley de Adquisiciones, Arrendamientos y Servicios del Sector Público" New law published in the Diario Oficial de la Federación (Official Gazette of the Federation) on January 4, 2000, last reform published DOF 10-11-2014.

[Cámara de Diputados del H. Congreso de la Unión, 2019] Cámara de Diputados del H. Congreso de la Unión, "Constitución Política de los Estados Unidos Mexicanos" Last reform published DOF 09-08-2019.

[Government of Canada, 2023] Government of Canada, "The procurement process" consulted in January 2023 https://buyandsell.gc.ca/for-businesses/selling-to-the-government-of-canada/the-procurement-process

[Smith, 1776] Smith A. "The Wealth of Nations" book 4, chapter 2, original title: "An Inquiry into the Nature and Causes of the Wealth of Nations" London, 1776.

Chapter 13

[ACM, 2023] Association for Computing Machinery, "ACM Code of Ethics and Professional Conduct," ACM, 2023, accessed January 2023 in https://www.acm.org/code-of-ethics

[AIS, 2022] Association for Information Systems, "AIS Code of Ethics and Professional Conduct," AIS, 2022, consulted in January 2023 in https://aisnet.org/page/MemberCodeOfConduct

[Andrews 1993] Andrews, P.; "Apple-Microsoft Lawsuit Fizzles To A Close -- 'Nothing Left' To Fight About"; The Seattle Times; Jun 2, 1993; Consulted in January 2023 in https://archive.seattletimes.com/archive/?date=19930602&slug=1704430

[BBC, 2022] BBC "Harvey Weinstein timeline: How the scandal unfolded" BBC, 24 October 2022, consulted in January 2023 in https://www.bbc.com/news/entertainment-arts-41594672

[Cámara de Diputados del H. Congreso de la Unión, 2021] Cámara de Diputados del H. Congreso de la Unión, "Código Civil Federal" last Reform, DOF, 11-01-2021, consulted in January 2023 in http://www.diputados.gob.mx/LeyesBiblio/pdf/2_110121.pdf

[Carranza, Robbins, and Dalby, 2019] Carranza, C.; Robbins, S.; and Dalby, C.; "Major Odebrecht Corruption Cases and Investigations in 2019" Insight Crime, 20 February 2019, consulted in January 2023 in https://insightcrime.org/news/analysis/major-latam-odebrecht-corruption-cases-investigations-2019/

[Coca-Cola, 2021] The Coca-Cola Company, "History" The Coca-Cola Company, 2021, consulted in January 2023 in https://www.coca-colacompany.com/company/history

[DiarioTI, 1998] DiarioTI, "IBM Alecciona a sus Subsidiarias Latinoamericanas" diarioTI.com, July 10, 1998, consulted January 2023 in https://diarioti.com/ibm-alecciona-a-sus-subsidiarias-latinoamericanas/6086

[e-tam.com.mx, 2015] e-tam.com.mx "Copyright", e-tam.com.mx, 2015, accessed January 2023 in http://www.e-tam.com.mx/website/public/derechos_autor

[Gunn, 1906] Gunn, B.G., "The Instruction of Ptah-Hotep" in "The Instruction of Ptah-Hotep and the Instruction of Ke' Gemini: The Oldest Books in the World" John Murray, Albemarle Street, Editor, London, England, 1906, accessed January 2023 in https://www.gutenberg.org/files/30508/30508-h/30508-h.htm

[IEEE, 2023] Institute of Electrical and Electronics Engineers, "IEEE Code of Ethics," IEEE, 2023, accessed January 2023 in https://www.ieee.org/about/corporate/governance/p7-8.html

[IMCP, 2015] Mexican Institute of Public Accountants, "Code of Professional Ethics," IMCP, 2015, accessed January 2023 in http://imcp.org.mx/wp-content/uploads/2015/12/Codigo_de_Etica_Profesional_10a_ed1.pdf

[IMPI 2013] Instituto Mexicano de la Propiedad Induatrial, Dirección Divisional de Patenets "Guía del Usuario de Patentes y Modelos de Utilidad" Secretaría de Economía, 2013, accessed January 2023 in https://sia.xoc.uam.mx/otc/documentos/guia_patentes_IMPI.pdf

[INDAUTOR, 2023] Instituto Nacional del Derecho de Autor "Registro Público del Derecho de Autor" Secretaría de Cultura, 2023. Consulted January 2023 in https://www.indautor.gob.mx/documentos/informacion-general/Registro.pdf

[Klainman, 2017] Klainman, Z. "Uber: The scandals that drove Travis Kalanick out" BBC, 21 June 2017, consulted in January 2023 https://www.bbc.com/news/technology-40352868

[Laudon & Laudon, 2019] Laudon, K.C., and Laudon, J.P. "Management Information Systems: Managing the Digital Firm," 16th edition, Pearson Education, 2019.

[Markoff, 1989] Markoff, J.; "Xerox vs. Apple: Standard 'Dashboard' Is at Issue," The New York Times, 20 December 1989, accessed December 2021 at https://www.nytimes.com/1989/12/20/business/xerox-vs-apple-standard-dashboard-is-at-issue.html

[Matute Urdaneta, 2016] Matute Urdaneta, G.; "Odebrecht scandal: US says 12 countries received bribes", CNN Español, December 22, 2016, consulted in January 2023 in https://cnnespanol.cnn.com/2016/12/22/escandalo-odebrecht-ee-uu-dice-que-12-paises-recibieron-sobornos/

[Ortiz Moreno, 1998] Ortiz Moreno, H.; "IBM will pay $37.5 million to the Attorney General's Office of Mexico City" La Jornada, 22 July 1998, consulted in January 2023 in https://www.jornada.com.mx/1998/07/23/pagara.html

[USPTO, 2023] US Patent and Trademark Office, "General information concerning patents," USPTO, 2023, accessed January 2023 in https://www.uspto.gov/patents/basics/general-information-patents

[USPTO, 2021] US Patent and Trademark Office, "Coronavirus Vaccine", USPTO, Pub. No.: US 2021/0379181 A1, Pub. Date: Dec, 9, 2021, consulted in January 2023 in https://image-ppubs.uspto.gov/dirsearch-public/print/downloadPdf/20210379181

[Wiener-Bronner, 2019] Wiener-Bronner, D.; "McDonald's CEO Steve Easterbrook is out for 'consensual relationship with an employee," CNN Business, 4 November 2019, accessed January 2023 in https://edition.cnn.com/2019/11/03/business/mcdonalds-ceo-steve-easterbrook-steps-down/index.html

[WIPO, 2023] World Intellectual Property Organization, "Patents: What is a Patent?", WIPO, 2023, accessed January 2023 in https://www.wipo.int/patents/en/

[WIPO, 2023-b] World Intellectual Property Organization, "Copyrights," WIPO, 2023, accessed January 2023 in https://www.wipo.int/copyright/en/

Chapter 14

[Belfort & Scorsese, 2013] Belfort, J. (writer) Scorsese, M., "The Wolf of Wall Street," Paramount Pictures, 2013.

[Bosworth, 1994] Bosworth, M.; "Solution Selling: Creating Buyers in Difficult Selling Markets"; ISBN: 978-0786303151; McGraw-Hill Companies; 1994.

[Budjac, 2017] Budjac, B. A.; "Conflict Management: A Practical Guide to Developing Negotiation Strategies"; ISBN: 978-9332543195; Pearson, 2017.

[Horowitz, 2023] Horowitz, L., "Sales Pipeline," TechTarget, accessed January 2023 in https://searchcustomerexperience.techtarget.com/definition/sales-pipeline

[Lewiki, Barry and Saunders, 2011] Lewiki, R. J., Barry, B. and Saunders, D.M., "Essentials of Negotiation"; Sixth Edition, ISBN:978-0-07-7862466, McGraw-Hill, New York, NY, 2011

[Rowe, 2001] Rowe, M., "The $2 Bargaining Simulation", Negotiation and conflict management, MIT, Spring 2001, accessed January 2023 in https://ocw.mit.edu/courses/sloan-school-of-management/15-667-negotiation-and-conflict-management-spring-2001/lecture-notes/gen_instr.pdf

[Rowe, 2002] Rowe, M.P., "Negotiation: Theory and Practice," MIT, Cambridge, MA, accessed January 2023 in https://ocw.mit.edu/courses/sloan-school-of-management/15-667-negotiation-and-conflict-management-spring-2001/study-materials/negotiation101.pdf

Chapter 15

[Burnett, 2012] Burnett, M., (Producer), "Shark Tank," Season 3, Episode 12, aired April 13, 2012.

[Laudon and Laudon, 2020] Laudon, K.C. and Laudon, J.P. "Management Information Systems: Managing the Digital Firm", 16th edition, ISBN: 978-0135191798, Pearson, 2020.

[Laudon and Traver, 2019] Laudon, K.C. and Traver C. G. "E-Commerce 2019: Business, Technology and Society," 15th edition, ISBN: 978-0134998459, Pearson, 2019.

[Nunno, Raskino, and Cox; 2021] Nunno, T.; Raskino, M.; and Cox, I; "Rules for Presenting Proposals to the Board of Directors for Transitioning Leaders"; Gartner; ID G00726339; Published May 1, 2020; Refreshed August 23, 2021.

[Turban, Volonino, and Wood, 2015] Turban, E.; Volonino, L.; Wood, G. R.; "Information technology for Management: digital strategies for insight, action and sustainable performance"; ISBN: 9781118897782; John Wiley & Sons, Hoboken, NJ, 2015.

[Volker and Phillips, 2018] Volker, J.; and Phillips, M.; "Six Points: A Plan for Success"; Journal of Management Policy & Practice; Vol. 19 Issue 1; 2018.

About the Author
Dr. Macedonio Alanís

alanis@tec.mx   maalanis@hotmail.com

Dr. Macedonio Alanis is Full Professor of Management Information Systems at Tecnologico de Monterrey (ITESM), in Monterrey, Mexico. He has published eight books and more than 120 papers, book chapters, and conferences on topics such as Digital Transformation, Business Intelligence, Strategic IT Management, and Educational Technology. He also designed and worked on a joint IT management program with Carnegie Mellon University and a joint specialization program in project management with Stanford University. Some of his classes, using distance learning, are attended live by nearly 1000 students in nine Latin American countries.

In the private sector, Dr. Alanis has been the CFO of Neoris, an IT company of the multinational CEMEX (NYSE: CX). He created Global Software Factory, a co-investment between CEMEX and World Software Services, developing IT projects in Mexico, Europe, the US, and South America. He has worked as a solutions architect for IBM and is part of Cutter Consortium's group of expert consultants.

In the public sector, he worked as CIO for the Government of the State of Nuevo Leon. He was elected president of CIAPEM, the national association of state and city CIOs in Mexico. He also participated in the definition of Mexico's national IT policies.

Dr. Alanis received the prestigious Eisenhower Fellowship and was elected to occupy the Americas Chair on the Association for Information Systems (AIS) Board of Directors.

Dr. Alanis holds a Ph.D. in Business Administration with a concentration on Management Information Systems from the University of Minnesota. He obtained a Master of Sciences in Computer Science (ScM) from Brown University and a BSc in Computer Science from Tecnologico de Monterrey in Monterrey, Mexico.

www.ingramcontent.com/pod-product-compliance
Lightning Source LLC
LaVergne TN
LVHW051227050326
832903LV00028B/2277